THE COMPLETE GUIDE TO STAFFORDSHIRE BULL TERRIERS

Dr Jo de Klerk

Publication Data

Dr Jo de Klerk

The Complete Guide to Staffordshire Bull Terriers ---- First edition.

Summary: "Successfully raising a Staffordshire Bull Terrier dog from puppy to old age" --- Provided by publisher.

ISBN: 978-1-07999-5-473

[1. Staffordshire Bull Terriers --- Non-Fiction] I. Title.

Design by Sorin Rădulescu

First paperback edition, 2019

TABLE OF CONTENTS

CHAPTER 1
Breed Overview

About the Breed

The Staffordshire Bull Terrier is one of the most popular breeds in the United Kingdom, with a strong following in the US, Canada, New Zealand, and other parts of the world. With its origins rooted in the dog fighting days of nineteenth-century industrial England, the breed tends to polarize public opinion. Many people still fear the Staffie, believing the breed to be dangerous. But others who have gotten to know the Staffordshire Bull Terrier through ownership will strongly defend the breed's reputation, arguing that the Staffie is a loyal and affectionate family dog with a radiant smile, and one of the few breeds recommended by the Kennel Club as safe around children.

Part of the problem leading to misconception surrounding the breed is that due to unregulated breeding from its origins and ever since, its exact genetic makeup can be inconsistent. Until recent years, traceable pedigrees have not existed. The breed is generally accepted to have arisen from the nineteenth-century Bull and Terrier, which was a Bulldog-Terrier cross, bred for the public spectacle of dog fighting. And when this breed was refined by selective breeding to become the English Bull Terrier, the Staffie eventually emerged from the original Bull and Terrier, only becoming recognized by the English Kennel Club in 1935, after which more regulated breeding created a breed standard.

The Staffordshire Bull Terrier, however, continues to suffer from casual breeding, which not only leads to it being severely overrepresented in animal rescue, but results in a wide variation of physical characteristics and temperaments. This means in many instances it is not possible to make generalizations about the breed. However, the advice given in this book takes the breed average as its model.

It should be noted that in the US, the American Staffordshire Terrier is marginally better known than the British Staffordshire Bull Terrier. Although both have ancestors in the Bull and Terrier, and both can be referred to as a "Staffie," these breeds are not the same. However, much of the advice given in this book will also apply to the Staffordshire Bull Terrier's American cousin.

*Photo Courtesy of
Karolina Bajer*

Looks

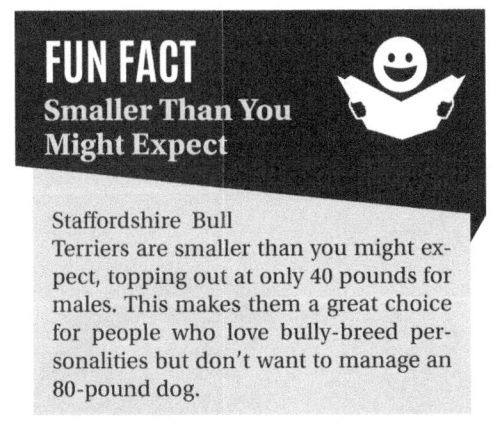

FUN FACT

Smaller Than You Might Expect

Staffordshire Bull Terriers are smaller than you might expect, topping out at only 40 pounds for males. This makes them a great choice for people who love bully-breed personalities but don't want to manage an 80-pound dog.

The Staffordshire Bull Terrier is a small to medium-sized breed, with a muscular build. Both his physical strength and his strength of character are disproportionate to his modest size. The Staffie is square set with a wide stance. With his short coat, every detail of the Staffie's musculature is defined, making him a popular traditional gentleman's dog. Even the Staffie's head appears muscled, with expressive folds between the eyes, and strong jaws set in a characteristic smile.

The Staffordshire Bull Terrier can be described as having an honest appearance, being little changed from the centuries-old original Bull and Terrier. In fact, being so similar to the original Old English Bulldog, which has since been bred beyond recognition, some argue the Staffie originates solely from that breed rather than having any Terrier in the mix. However, due to the unregistered nature of the Staffie's origins, today's breed will have mixed genetics, but the Kennel Club breed standard helps to set a blueprint for the dog's appearance.

Staffies can vary greatly in size, but usually measure 14-16 inches (35-40cm) in height at the withers. Male Staffordshire Bull Terriers are larger than females at 28-38lb (13-17kg), with females typically weighing 24-34lb (11-16kg). There is a wide variety of coat colors, including red, fawn, white, black or blue (gray). Another popular variation, brindle, is a close combination of black and brown hair colors, and can vary in shade. It gives a polished walnut appearance or sometimes a tiger stripe. Staffies are sometimes a solid color, but more commonly have white on their chest, paws, head, or nose. The Kennel Club will accept any of these wide variations, but black and tan or liver color are not favored in the showing world.

Photo Courtesy of Karolina Bajer

Age Expectancy

The Staffordshire Bull Terrier typically lives for over 12 years, and although the breed can suffer from a range of health conditions detailed in Chapter 13, this book aims to help your dog live his allotted years in good health and to the full.

Personality

The most striking characteristic of the Staffie is his big smile, and this really does represent the huge affection the breed holds for his human family. The Staffie is full of energy and fun, and life is never dull with a Staffie around. Many people who have owned Staffies take the breed to their heart so much that they would never have any other breed, which demonstrates how misunderstood the Staffordshire Bull Terrier is in popular perception. Staffie owners also typically say that their dog thinks he is human! Although this may be true of many dog breeds, it does illustrate the special bond the Staffie shares with his people. As far as other dogs go, however, the Staffie can take them or leave them.

FUN FACT

The "Children's Nursemaid"

In Britain, the Staffordshire Bull Terrier is often referred to as the "children's nursemaid" thanks to its gentle nature with (human) children. Still, it's important to note that no dog of any breed should be left alone with children.

Staffies are full of energy and exuberance. They may be too much for some people, so careful consideration should be given to whether the family can cope with such a boisterous breed. On the whole, females will be quieter than male Staffies, and less reactive. However, if you are selecting a puppy, you will only see his true personality come out as he grows up, and can only make an educated guess from his bloodlines if he has a registered pedigree. But early training and socialization, as set out in Chapters 5, 6, and 7, can help to make sure your dog's personality develops along the right lines. If adopting an adult dog from rescue, you know what you are getting, as the dog will have had a full assessment. However, you may have some behavioral issues to deal with from your dog's previous bad experiences, or neglect of his training.

With your love and care, your Staffie's innate sunny personality will come out as he grows in trust and respect for you as his special person.

Inside the home

Photo Courtesy of
Christine Wilson

The Staffordshire Bull Terrier is thin-coated and human-oriented, which makes him unsuited to living full-time outside in the yard. He would much prefer to live by your side in your home. The trouble is that the breed can be very boisterous, which can be a problem in a confined space, especially if you have children. Also, Staffies are easily bored due to their high intelligence, and can become destructive. Some tips to address this are given in Chapter 5.

Crate training a Staffie from puppyhood is a good idea with this breed. A puppy will grow to see his crate as his safe space. It will help him feel secure, but at the same time, it also gives the family time out occasionally from his high-energy antics. If you have adopted a rescue dog that is not used to a crate, he may not take to it right away or even at all, but making a crate available with an open door as his "den" may lead to acceptance.

You can read more about preparing your home for a Staffordshire Bull Terrier in Chapter 3.

Outside the home

It has already been said that Staffordshire Bull Terriers are full of energy, so access to a secure yard is a must. In your yard your dog will be able to let off steam and engage in natural dog behavior, as well as toilet appropriately.

Staffies also need regular exercise and the opportunity to socialize. They are not necessarily natural at this, and making friends with other dogs can be a learning process. Some tips for this are given in Chapter 7.

*Photo Courtesy of
Emma Ceely*

One problem many Staffie owners experience outside the home is that when walking their dog in public places, some people can be fearful of the breed due to its negative reputation and the dog's bullish appearance. This makes it doubly important with the Staffordshire Bull Terrier that he is trained to show the world how well behaved the breed can be. Obedience training in particular will earn your dog public approval, and some tips are given in Chapter 6. However, obedience classes are highly recommended, as they combine training with the opportunity for socialization in a controlled environment.

Finally, if you do find yourself with a dog that has aggression issues either with strangers or other dogs, it is your legal responsibility to muzzle him when out in public.

Exercise Requirements

"Your Stafford will love to exercise so developing a consistent weekly routine is good for them, as well as your family. Remember all Staffords can be heat and cold sensitive so make sure they get access to plenty of water (NOT all at once) in hot months."

Robert Randall
Guardstock Staffordshire Bull Terriers

The Staffordshire Bull Terrier's exuberance means that he needs plenty of opportunity to burn off energy in the form of walks and play. But it is possible to overwalk a Staffie as while he has great stamina, he is prone to overheating. The Kennel Club recommends an hour a day for an adult Staffie. A puppy should be walked for only 15-30 minutes daily while their bones and joints are developing. However, as the Staffordshire Bull Terrier is not naturally inclined to get on with other dogs, if you wish to walk him in the park he will need socialization training. Many Staffie owners find secure dog fields very beneficial for this breed, as their dogs can be off-leash in a safe environment. In addition, some Staffie owners take part in canine sports such as obedience and agility to focus their dog's mind as well as keep him fit. The Staffordshire Bull Terrier is an intelligent dog so his brain needs exercise as well as his body; then he will happily snuggle up in the evening and dream about his day!

Photo Courtesy of
Helen Nolan

Costs of Keeping a Staffordshire Bull Terrier

The Staffordshire Bull Terrier is a pedigree breed, and if you are purchasing a puppy from a registered breeder, you can expect to pay in excess of $1,000. However, the lifetime cost of a pedigree Staffie is likely to be less than one from a backyard breeder, as he should have been bred to be free of genetic diseases, and with a healthy conformation.

If you are adopting a Staffie from a shelter, you will still have a rehoming fee to pay, which may be several hundred dollars, and goes to meet some of the costs your dog will have incurred, such as kenneling, neutering, transport, vaccinations, microchipping, parasite treatment, food, and any veterinary costs.

On a daily basis, your Staffie's costs are average. He is a small to medium breed with a moderate appetite, and although the breed can suffer from specific health conditions, Staffies are generally healthy. Veterinary insurance, however, is a sensible precaution that will help you to budget, so that you never have to face any huge veterinary bills for an accident or serious illness. Public liability insurance is also essential, and is usually included in pet insurance.

Some of the equipment you will need for your Staffie is listed in Chapter 3. However, what you choose to spend is largely a personal decision. Those on a tight budget may choose just to purchase the essentials, many of which can be found secondhand. Other owners may love to indulge their dog as it gives them pleasure to do so.

If you are planning to welcome a Staffie into your life, you are in for a lot of fun, undivided loyalty, and loads of unconditional affection! But there will be challenges along the way. With a bit of planning, you can make sure the ride is as smooth as it can possibly be, and that your Staffie grows to show the world that he is everything a family dog should be!

CHAPTER 2
Breed History

Origin of the breed

The Staffordshire Bull Terrier that we know today as a loyal family dog has its origins in a very different, more brutal world, and tracing its earliest ancestors takes us right back to eighteenth-century England, where blood sports were a form of popular entertainment.

The Bull and Terrier

The word "Bull" in the Staffordshire Bull Terrier's name comes from the Old English Bulldog that went into the genetic mix. Bulldogs were bred to bait bulls. They were fearless and would take on a bull, ostensibly to tenderize the meat, but in reality, the entertainment brought to a bloodthirsty crowd was the real draw. Bull baiting and bear baiting led to setting dogs upon each other in the pit, but the entertainment value of two Bulldogs engaged in a fight was limited, as the Bulldog was designed simply to "go low, pin, and hold," with no action other than two dogs gripping each other. So a new breed of fighting dog was developed, by crossing the Bulldog with the tenacious English Terrier for a more exciting fight, with greater speed and variety in the attack. There were various forms of Terrier in England at the time, bred for hunting down vermin, and it was already recognized that introducing Bulldog blood into the Terrier made this little hunting breed more resilient to the bites it would receive in its job. In crossing the Bulldog and the Terrier for the pit, a fearless and tenacious breed was developed known as the "Bull and Terrier." This new breed, which no longer belonged to either foundation breed, was bred for "gameness," meaning it was feisty and would take on anything. The Bull and Terrier would become the founding ancestor of

FUN FACT
Descended from War Dogs

The Staffordshire Bull Terrier is descended from giant Molossian war dogs that the Greeks used in battle. These Molossian war dogs also gave birth to Mastiff breeds and Great Danes, among other dog breeds.

Photo Courtesy of Courtney Ryder

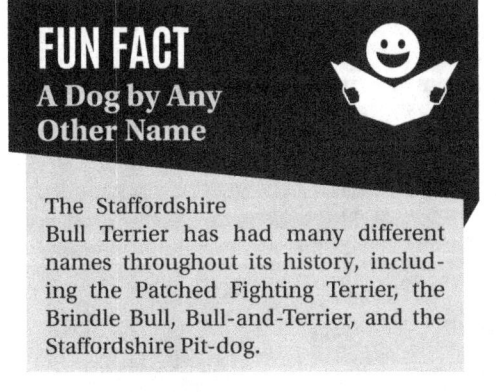

FUN FACT

A Dog by Any Other Name

The Staffordshire Bull Terrier has had many different names throughout its history, including the Patched Fighting Terrier, the Brindle Bull, Bull-and-Terrier, and the Staffordshire Pit-dog.

the American Pit Bull Terrier, the Miniature Bull Terrier, the English Bull Terrier, the American Staffordshire Terrier, and the Staffordshire Bull Terrier.

The Bull and Terrier was originally known by several different names, one of which was simply the Bull Terrier. However, this name later became associated with a distinct offshoot of the breed developed by James Hinks that we now know as the English Bull Terrier. This line was a cross between the Bull and Terrier and the English White Terrier, and originally was bred to be pure white in color. The modern English Bull Terrier has a distinctive curved head and triangular eyes. The Staffordshire Bull Terrier, on the other hand, remained true to the original Bull and Terrier, to which it bears a greater resemblance than James Hinks' English Bull Terrier. However, more recently, Staffordshire Bull Terrier blood has been introduced back into the English Bull Terrier to produce other color variants less susceptible to the genetic problems of a pure white breed.

The Bull and Terrier was quite a broad term with regional variations depending on the local stock of dogs chosen for crossing. The Staffordshire Bull Terrier that we know today originated from the Cradley Heath type that had more Bulldog blood. In fact, one lesser-held theory is that the Staffordshire Bull Terrier had no terrier blood at all, but was derived from selective breeding of the original Old English Bulldog. This is unlikely, given the successful introduction of Terrier qualities in the Bull and Terrier breed and the unregulated breeding at the time, but demonstrates how the Bulldog genetics are more evident in the Staffordshire Bull Terrier.

In 1835, baiting was made illegal in the United Kingdom, as was dog fighting, but being easier to conceal, it became the main focus of bloodsport entertainment, and was popular also in the US with the introduction of the Bull and Terrier. Apart from gambling, it was also used to refine the breed as dogs would fight to the death, so only the strongest and fittest would survive. But alongside the desired aggression toward other dogs, the fighting dog would have to be trustworthy with its handler and the judge. This character trait has survived through all the breed modifications that make up today's Staffordshire Bull Terrier, which is renowned for the loyalty it shows toward its owner and its non-aggressive quality toward humans, even though it can still be reactive with other dogs.

The Modern Staffordshire Bull Terrier

In 1911, the law was tightened in regard to illegal dog fighting in the United Kingdom. In any case, James Hinks had developed his line of Bull Terriers in the mid-nineteenth century as a gentleman's breed, and the association with dog fighting was beginning to diminish. It wasn't until the 1930s that the modern Staffordshire Bull Terrier was developed with the aim of Kennel Club recognition, led by breeders Joseph Dunn and Joe Mallen, who founded the Cradley Heath Club, a small band of working men who met at the Cross Guns in England's West Midlands, known as the Black Country. Amongst this community, dog fighting was a way of life, and dogs were bred to work hard and fight hard, and as status symbols. But these men were serious about the quality of their dogs and set about proving them at Crufts, winning awards, challenge certificates, and, in 1935, recognition by the Kennel Club, which approved the name Staffordshire Bull Terrier. In 1939 Gentleman Jim became the first ever Staffordshire Bull Terrier Supreme Champion.

The period around the Second World War was the point at which the Staffordshire Bull Terrier became established as a recognized breed, and modern purebred lines will trace their ancestry back to the chief stud dogs, Fearless Joe (J-line), Game Lad (L-line), Brindle Mick (M-line), Rum Bot-

Photo Courtesy of Helena Lehtis

tle (B-line), Ribchester Bob (R-line), and Cinderbank Beauty through Togo (C-line or sometimes referred to as the T-line).

With the elevation in status due to recognition by the Kennel Club, and through the emergence of the breed as a family dog and loyal companion rather than a fighting dog, the Staffordshire Bull Terrier has grown in popularity over recent decades. Not only does the Staffie look glossy and beautiful, but the breed is full of personality and loves his people unconditionally. The American Kennel Club sums up the transformation in the Staffie by stating, "Happily, good breeding transformed this former gladiator into a mild, playful companion with a special feel for kids." This popularity, however, has been both positive and negative for the Staffordshire Bull Terrier.

Breed-Specific Legislation

In becoming one of the most popular breeds in the United Kingdom, US, and many other countries, The Staffordshire Bull Terrier has become a victim of its own popularity, suffering from indiscriminate overbreeding, unregistered breeding from poor stock, cross-breeding with Pit Bull types, and a negative association with antisocial subculture. Consequently, the breed has become seriously overrepresented in rescue shelters, with the result that unwanted and untrained dogs can demonstrate negative behaviors, and the breed's reputation has become tarnished as a result.

Because of this, some organizations in the UK have lobbied to have the Staffordshire Bull Terrier added to the list of banned breeds covered by the 1991 Dangerous Dogs Act. However, this idea has been consistently rejected to date. In fact, like the American Kennel Club, the English Kennel Club goes so far as to recommend the breed as one of the few suitable to be around children.

In the US, the Staffordshire Bull Terrier is classified as a Pit Bull type. The Pit Bull is a banned breed in the US, although the application of the law varies between individual states. The degree of Pit Bull in any Staffordshire Bull Terrier will always be a matter of contention, with the smaller English Staffordshire Bull Terrier being less Pit Bull in appearance and temperament than its distant cousin, the larger American Staffordshire Terrier. These two distinct breeds are often confused, and with so many gray areas in breed-specific legislation across the world, the Staffie continues to be misunderstood and vulnerable to the vagaries of the law.

The American Staffordshire Terrier

The larger American Staffordshire Terrier is not the same dog as the English Staffordshire Bull Terrier, though both have the same nineteenth-century British ancestor in the Bull and Terrier. The American Staffordshire Terrier was bred from the American Pit Bull Terrier, whose ancestors came from the Walsall type of English Bull and Terriers, brought over by immigrants to the United States in the mid-nineteenth century. The American Staffordshire Terrier is also known as the Amstaff, but also sometimes as the Staffie, resulting in some confusion between the American and English Staffordshire Bull Terrier. Although the Amstaff is not a banned breed in the UK or the US, it may be taken for assessment under breed-specific legislation if it is perceived to be of Pit Bull appearance. Dogs assessed as Pit Bull may be exempted and released back to their owners under certain restrictions if they can be proven to be non-aggressive.

Photo Courtesy of Karen Kilpatrick

This book focuses on the English Staffordshire Bull Terrier; however, much of its content will also apply to its American cousin.

The English Staffordshire Bull Terrier Breed Standard (AKC 1990)

General Appearance: The Staffordshire Bull Terrier is a smooth-coated dog. It should be of great strength for its size and, although muscular, should be active and agile.

Size, Proportion, Substance: Height at shoulder - 14 to 16 inches. Weight - Dogs, 28 to 38 pounds; bitches, 24 to 34 pounds, these heights being related to weights. Non-conformity with these limits is a fault. In proportion, the length of back, from withers to tail set, is equal to the distance from withers to ground.

Photo Courtesy of
Daniel Pickering
Photo by Diamond Dogs Fine Art Pet Photography

Head: Short, deep through, broad skull, very pronounced cheek muscles, distinct stop, short foreface, black nose. Pink (Dudley) nose to be considered a serious fault. Eyes - Dark preferable, but may bear some relation to coat color. Round, of medium size, and set to look straight ahead. Light eyes or pink eye rims to be considered a fault, except that where the coat surrounding the eye is white the eye rim may be pink. Ears - Rose or half-pricked and not large. Full drop or full prick to be considered a serious fault. Mouth - A bite in which the outer side of the lower incisors touches the inner side of the upper incisors. The lips should be tight and clean. The badly undershot or overshot bite is a serious fault.

Neck, Topline, Body: The neck is muscular, rather short, clean in outline and gradually widening toward the shoulders. The body is close coupled, with a level topline, wide front, deep brisket and well sprung ribs being rather light in the loins. The tail is undocked, of medium length, low set, tapering to a point and carried rather low. It should not curl much and may be likened to an old-fashioned pump handle. A tail that is too long or badly curled is a fault.

Forequarters: Legs straight and well boned, set rather far apart, without looseness at the shoulders and showing no weakness at the pasterns, from which point the feet turn out a little. Dewclaws on the forelegs may be removed. The feet should be well padded, strong and of medium size.

Photo Courtesy of Lucy Whitmore

Hindquarters: The hindquarters should be well muscled, hocks let down with stifles well bent. Legs should be parallel when viewed from behind. Dewclaws, if any, on the hind legs are generally removed. Feet as in front.

Coat: Smooth, short and close to the skin, not to be trimmed or de-whiskered.

Color: Red, fawn, white, black or blue, or any of these colors with white. Any shade of brindle or any shade of brindle with white. Black-and-tan or liver color to be disqualified.

Gait: Free, powerful and agile with economy of effort. Legs moving parallel when viewed from front or rear. Discernible drive from hind legs.

Temperament: From the past history of the Staffordshire Bull Terrier, the modern dog draws its character of indomitable courage, high intelligence, and tenacity. This, coupled with its affection for its friends, and children in particular, its off-duty quietness and trustworthy stability, makes it a foremost all-purpose dog.

Disqualification: *Black-and-tan or liver color.*

CHAPTER 3
Preparations for a New Dog

If you have owned dogs of any breed before, you will already know what you will need for your new dog and how to adapt your home for the new arrival. But if this is your first dog, you may be anxious to make sure you have thought of everything before your dog arrives, so that he will feel welcome and slot straight into family life. This chapter will help you prepare your home, with special consideration given to the size and temperament of a Staffordshire Bull Terrier.

Preparing Your Home for a Pet

Many people believe, and rightly so, that a house is not a home without a dog. Your Staffordshire Bull Terrier will certainly bring a lot of love and fun into your home. He is also sure to fill a space disproportionate to his modest size! The other consideration, as with any dog, is that they will be spending a certain amount of the day outside, for exercise and to toilet. So they will be bringing some of the outdoors into your house, as well as shedding their coat. Happily, the Staffie is not a profuse shedder, neither does he have a long coat to attract dirt. However, if you are used to having an immaculate house, you will need to accept that this will take a lot more work to maintain, or adopt a slightly more relaxed standard when your dog arrives. Realistic expectations are only fair for your dog.

It is perfectly acceptable to keep certain rooms off-limits to your new dog. Many owners like to do this, especially if they have young children and would like to keep a relaxed and safe, dog-free play area. And whether or not your new dog is allowed in the bedrooms or upstairs is a matter of preference. However, if you have children, it can be advisable from the get-go to make the bedrooms out of bounds to the dog, so that the dog does not see himself as above the children in the family hierarchy. There is more about

HELPFUL TIP
Indoor or Outdoor Dog?

While images of bully breeds living outdoors on chains are common, they do best living indoors with their family. They have been bred as companions for more than a century and don't do well being banished to the yard.

Photo Courtesy of
Helena Lehtis

Photo Courtesy of
Amber Moore

this in Chapter 7. Setting the ground rules from the very start sends a clear message to your dog that he will naturally accept, rather than placing new restrictions on him further down the line. So, with this in mind, you may need to invest in some stair gates to section off any parts of your home to which you do not wish your dog to have access.

Once you have decided which rooms your dog will be allowed in, you need to look for any hazards that might present themselves to a new dog, especially if you are bringing home a puppy that will chew everything. And if you have any precious things, these should be put out of the dog's reach. Hazards may include the TV remote, or anything with batteries that could be ingested, poisonous house plants, soft furnishings with stuffing that could easily be swallowed, fragile ornaments, even things like chocolate, medicines, or chewing gum containing xylitol that might be lying around, as these are toxic to your dog.

You will need to decide whether or not your dog will be allowed on the sofa. Many owners love to snuggle up with their dogs on the sofa, where-as others would prefer their couch to stay clean. It is a matter of personal choice and there is no wrong or right option, but you need to be consistent from the outset. If your dog will have access to your sofa when you are out, you cannot expect him to resist temptation in your absence, so the battle will be constantly undermined. Therefore, if you wish to train your dog to stay off the sofa, you would need to shut him in a room such as the kitchen, or in a safe and secure yard, or in his crate when you leave him, at least until such time as he knows and respects the rules.

If you are happy to share your sofa with your dog, it makes sense for it to be an older sofa that you will not be worried about, and well made to resist chewing. Old leather sofas can be easier to wipe clean than textile, although loose covers are a good idea as they can be washed. Some people like to use throws to protect their furniture.

Likewise, hard floors in the rooms to which your dog has access will make cleaning much easier, especially at the housebreaking stage. However, if you already have carpet, it is worth investing in a carpet shampooing machine from the outset. Then when your dog has the inevitable little accidents, they can be promptly cleaned and sanitized without fuss.

It is a great idea to have a crate for your dog's use inside the home and in a vehicle, more of which is discussed in Chapter 8. Contrary to some people's opinions, a crate is not a prison, but a sanctuary to a dog. It can be very comforting for a dog to have his own safe space. You can make your dog's crate into a cozy den by putting in a bed or clean towels, and some toys or safe chews. If you are preparing for a puppy, it can be very useful to crate train your dog from the start, because being able to shut the door to the crate without upsetting your dog means you can leave him in there happily while you are out, and he will be safe and not destroying the house. Also, if you have house guests that do not like dogs, you can contain your four-legged friend for a while. Plus, if you ever have to board your dog with a friend or pet sitter, he has his own special place where he will settle for the night, and not make a nuisance of himself!

Crate training at the puppy stage also makes housebreaking easier, as dogs are naturally disposed to keep clean in their bed, so your dog will hold his bladder and bowels in his crate, and relieve himself promptly when let outside. There is more about housebreaking in Chapter 5.

If you are adopting a rescue dog, possibly with emotional scars, he may or may not take to the crate in the early stages. If he shows any anxiety, he should never be shut in, but should simply have access to the crate as a cozy safe space where he has a bed, toys and chews, even the occasional treat, and can come and go as he pleases.

Metal crates are the best bet for Staffordshire Bull Terriers, as whether you are buying a puppy or adopting a rescue dog, they can chew and be destructive. You can cover a metal crate with a towel or blanket to make it cozy and keep out drafts. If you are adopting an adult Staffie that you know to be non-destructive, then a textile crate is another option.

If you do not wish to use a crate, or you wish your dog to sleep in a bed positioned elsewhere at night, now is the time to think where you might put this. Some options might be in the living room, in the kitchen, in the hallway, on the upstairs landing, or in the bedroom. This is a matter of personal choice. It can make life easier for the future if your dog does not sleep in the bedroom; for example, if you go away and have to employ pet sitters or board your dog in someone else's home. Also, it discourages your dog from challenging the family hierarchy if he sleeps downstairs, and it keeps your own sleeping environment cleaner. In the short term, however, you may encounter some whines or barks of protest at your choice until your dog is settled into a routine.

If you crave the companionship of a dog snuggled on your own bed at night, your personal and family situation is unlikely to change, and you have a tolerant pet sitter when you go away, then this is a choice some dog owners make. However, it is not so easy to undo this choice later on.

The next thing you should consider when preparing your home for a new dog is the security of your yard. Even if you already have a dog, your

Photo Courtesy of Holly Arrow

new Staffie may find ways and means of escape that are not on your existing dog's radar. For example, your Staffie will grow to be a medium-sized athletic dog, capable of jumping. So three-foot-high fences that contain a small dog will not be a challenge for your Staffie, and six feet is recommended. Also, your Staffie may dig, so the fence should go all the way to the ground. If you are buying a puppy, he will also be able to squeeze through any small gaps or under gates, so these should be blocked up, and if you have palisade or picket fencing, the gaps should be infilled with wire mesh.

Preparing Your Home for a Guard Dog

Most people choose a Staffordshire Bull Terrier as a companion and family dog. The Staffie is not naturally aggressive, but he can look intimidating and of course, the breed still has a fighting reputation, however undeserved. For these reasons, some owners will choose a Staffie for protection.

It is not within the scope of this book to discuss the use of the Staffordshire Bull Terrier as an attack dog, which is a specialist field that should never be entered into by an inexperienced owner. If your circumstances require such a dog, you should seek professional advice.

On the other hand, the Staffie can be taught to guard a property simply by barking at the presence of an intruder. Staffies are suited to this job because they are very protective toward their people, loyal, confident, and easy to train. They are also non-aggressive to humans, which is an asset, as when a dog attacks and causes harm to another person, even an intruder, it can result in a criminal prosecution and possible destruction of the dog.

The very fact that you own a Staffie, which is a breed that sits near the gray area of breed-specific legislation, means that you should put a "Beware of Dog" sign on your gate, even if your dog is a pussy cat. The sign and your dog's muscular appearance may deter intruders in itself. Even though it seems petty, if an intruder did receive a bite, you would be less liable to prosecution if you had a sign.

When your dog comes home, as an additional part of his training, you will teach him his territory, and defensive techniques such as alert barking and standing guard. But it is important he should be well socialized and have plenty of exposure to environments outside the confines of his territory as well.

Photo Courtesy of
Ashley Heron

Shopping List

For many new owners, a trip to the pet store to buy all the things their new dog needs is part of the exciting build-up to bringing home their new companion. Other owners, however, may be on a budget, and careful only to buy the essentials. If you are bringing home a puppy, obviously your dog will grow, and some of the things you will buy for him at this stage may not be suitable further down the line.

When you pick up your dog, you will need to take with you a collar and leash. Alternatively, you can take a rope slip-leash, which you pop over the head of your dog. This is a popular choice for a Staffordshire Bull Terrier as it stays snug on the neck and the dog is less likely to back out of it like a collar if it is too loose. However, a collar is also important, as you can attach an identity tag which will help you be reunited with your dog if he should escape or stray. It is worth preparing an ID tag with your contact details before you pick up your dog, as he is most vulnerable to escaping in the early weeks while he gets to know you. Make sure the collar has a wide range of adjustment if you are getting a puppy as he will grow fast.

A harness is also a good purchase, as provided it is well-fitting your dog will not be able to escape from it when on the leash. A harness is also kinder to the dog than leading off a collar as if he pulls, the tension is diverted across the chest rather than straining the delicate bones of the neck. Ultimately though, your Staffie will be trained to walk nicely on a loose leash, and to have excellent recall to enjoy off-leash romps. As a fashion accessory, the Staffordshire Bull Terrier is traditionally seen in a leather harness, and often a studded leather collar. But while he is a puppy, softer textile products with plenty of adjustability are more suitable.

Choke chains are not recommended even though the full-choke and half-choke may have a traditional association with the breed. This is because they are harsh, and these days, positive reinforcement is accepted as the best method to train a companion dog. There is more about this in Chapters 5 and 6.

It has already been mentioned that a crate is a good purchase, and a metal crate will withstand any chewing or clawing at the sides. You may wish to purchase two crates if you are also going to use this method to travel your dog in the car. Your Staffie is unlikely to need a crate any bigger than medium size. Dogs prefer the secure feeling of a crate that is not too large compared to their size. Also, if you are using a crate for housebreaking, the dog should not have so much space that he can soil at the other end of the

Photo Courtesy of
Lauren Vitalo

crate away from his bed, as that is defeating the object. Having said that, your puppy will grow quickly, so a small crate may not last him very long.

Your dog will need a bed unless you are intending to use towels or blankets in his crate. When purchasing a bed for a puppy, it is worth bearing in mind that he will chew for the first year of his life as he explores his new world and his milk teeth give way to his adult teeth. So, a plastic bed is your best bet, and you can line it with old towels for his comfort which can be washed regularly. As with the crate, do not choose anything too large, as your puppy will like to feel secure. In any case, when he reaches his adult size and has gotten past the destructive stage, you may wish to choose a softer, more luxurious bed for him.

Your new dog will need a bowl for his food and another for his water. Heavy stoneware bowls are a good choice, since they cannot be tipped or pushed around the floor. A plastic bowl for travel is also useful.

Before you stock up on any food for your dog, check with the breeder or rescue center what your dog is already on. The first weeks with you are a big change in his life, and it is worth keeping his diet consistent at this stage to prevent any tummy upsets. If you decide to change him onto another food at a later stage, be sure to introduce it slowly by combining it incrementally with his existing food.

If you have reached the checkout of the pet store with just the items on this list – well done! There is such an array of products to choose from, and many owners love to indulge their dogs. There is certainly nothing wrong with that. But your dog doesn't know if his things have a designer label, as long as they are safe and clean, they fit him well, and are suitable for his life stage.

Now your house is ready for your dog, you can look forward to the day you bring him home!

CHAPTER 4

How to Choose a Staffordshire Bull Terrier

Once you have decided that a Staffordshire Bull Terrier is the breed for you, you will need to decide where to find your new best friend. Broadly speaking, there are two distinct approaches and much depends on whether you want a puppy or would prefer to rehome an adult dog.

Purchasing or Rescuing?

In general, if you want to welcome a puppy into your family, you will be looking at purchasing from a breeder. There can be an exception to this rule, given that Staffordshire Bull Terriers are greatly overrepresented in rescue. It can occur when a pregnant female is brought into a rescue center, or a litter of puppies are found that have been dumped. So, if you are really drawn to adopting a dog in desperate need of a home, but you really want a puppy, it is worth contacting the rescue centers in your area, as they may well have Staffie pups available. Bear in mind, though, that a rescue puppy will almost always come with no history, and the health and temperament of the parents will be unknown. Also, your puppy may not cost you any less than buying from a registered breeder as all rescues charge a rehoming fee. And in the long term, any issues arising from poor breeding may cost you more.

Many people will gladly take the risk of adopting a rescue pup because of the satisfaction in giving that dog a brighter future, and taking a chance on future costs is not an issue. On the other hand, if you prefer to take on a known quantity, or you wish to

HELPFUL TIP
Do Your Research

A well-bred and well-socialized Staffordshire Bull Terrier is likely to be a healthy, happy, friendly dog. A Staffy that comes from a puppy mill or backyard breeder is more likely to be sick and aggressive, so put in the time to find a reputable breeder. Alternatively, there are lots of bully-breed dogs, including Staffies, in your local shelter that may make great pets; just make sure to choose a shelter or rescue group that does behavior testing, so you have a better idea of what you're getting into.

Photo Courtesy of
Zoe Butler

show your dog or breed from him or her, buying a Staffordshire Bull Terrier from a registered breeder is a sound choice.

Some people prefer to adopt an older dog, especially as there are so many Staffies in rescue. This can be very rewarding, as for many of these dogs that have been rejected, all it takes is a bit of love and a settled home environment to turn their lives around. For other dogs, the job may be more of a challenge. Staffies are not aggressive or disobedient by nature, but if they have experienced cruelty or neglect, it may be a longer job to restore their trust. In severe cases, behavioral issues can be so engrained that they can only be improved to a certain point, beyond which they have to be managed. This can impact severely on the owner's life, so a rescue dog is not to be taken on lightly. However, in most cases, a rescued Staffie will reward his adopter with a lifetime of gratitude for giving him a second chance, as Staffies really know how to form a bond, more than most other breeds of dog.

Researching the Establishment

Photo Courtesy of Shannon Freeman

The Staffordshire Bull Terrier is a breed that has been badly overbred, and a lot of breeding is casual, accidental, and unregistered. Therefore, you may find pups for sale on the internet or advertised locally. In some instances, you may even be able to see the parents. However, you should be very savvy about back street breeders, or puppy farms, masquerading as reputable owners who have happened to have a litter born to their family dog. You may be shown the puppies in a clean front room of a family house, unaware of the squalid conditions their overbred dogs are kept in elsewhere. You may be given false information about the parents, and any paperwork may not be valid. The dogs will not be registered if the parents are not, and therefore you will not be able to show your dog or breed a registered litter from him or her. Most significantly, your dog may carry or develop a number of genetic conditions that affect the Staffordshire Bull Terrier. Some of these are outlined in Chapter 13.

To avoid being caught in this situation, you should look for a breeder that is registered with the Kennel Club in your country. Their website is a good place to start. Alternatively, most registered breeders advertise online, giving you the opportunity to research that breeder's dogs, and check that they have the bloodlines, appearance, temperament, and qualities that you are looking for.

Buying a Staffie as a puppy means that you are in full control of his training right from his early socialization, through to obedience training and any further activities that you may have in mind for your dog. Your dog will always have known kindness and will form an early bond with you as his owner. Therefore, he will be a settled dog and likely to grow into a typical happy, loyal, and gentle-natured Staffordshire Bull Terrier.

Inquire about the Parents

If you have identified a registered breeder or a number of breeders on the Kennel Club website, or elsewhere online, that have litters available or expected, then you are in a good position to research the parents before you even visit the breeder for the first time. This is because parents with registered bloodlines have most likely excelled in shows, or their bloodline has certain distinguishing characteristics, and these can be researched on the internet.

Breeding to approved Kennel Club standards requires certain protocols to ensure the health of the puppies, and this involves testing the parents for certain hereditary conditions. Only those parents that do not carry these conditions may be bred from. In this way, by purchasing from a registered breeder, you can have a good degree of confidence that your dog will remain healthy throughout a long life. Therefore, even if your purchase cost is initially higher, a dog with registered breeding will usually cost you less in the long run because he will not be a frequent visitor to the vet's office.

Beginning with the mother of the puppies, you should check that she has not been bred prior to her third season, and that she is not over seven years of age. She should also not have bred more than three litters. You should be able to see the mother as she may be with the puppies, or at least on the same premises, depending on which stage of the weaning process the puppies are at. However, the father is often a stud dog that lives with another owner, so unless you make an appointment to visit him, you may have to make do with photographs and copies of his documentation.

You should ask the breeder to show you certificates for the health tests and screening that have been done for both parents. These tests are optional, and the breeder should be able to explain why he may not have tested for every condition.

At the very least, the parents should have been scored for hip and elbow dysplasia, and have been screened for hereditary cataract (HC). For a Staffordshire Bull Terrier, the hip score should be lower than the breed mean score of 12.9, and the elbow score should be as low as possible and ideally 0:0.

You should also ask the breeder about the medical history of the parents, grandparents, and great-grandparents of the puppies, in case there are any other diseases in the family line for which there is currently no genetic or screening test available. You should ask the breeder about their policy in the case of any genetic disease occurring to your dog later on in its

*Photo Courtesy of
Shanae Rumbel*

life. Some breeders may agree to contribute to medical costs or refund the purchase price. At the very least, a good breeder will want to be informed if any genetic condition should arise, to improve their breeding decisions.

Finally, you should look at the five-generation pedigree certificate of the puppy, for instances of the same name appearing more than once. When this occurs, it is a sign of inbreeding, and any genetic weaknesses can be magnified. It is not uncommon for pedigree dogs to have some names cropping up more than once; however, it is considered responsible practice by the Kennel Club that inbreeding should be limited.

Looking at the Puppy

Breeders generally welcome visits from potential purchasers after the puppies are four weeks of age, with a view to releasing the pups at around ten weeks when they are fully weaned. Initially, the puppies' characters may not be evident, so the first visit may not be the time to make your selection, but by 6-8 weeks you will be able to see their different personalities. The breeder may wish to make his own first personal selection at this stage to continue the breeding line. Others may also have reserved pups before you, so do check to save disappointment.

Sometimes a breeder will make his own choice about which pup goes to which owner on the waiting list, based on his evaluation of the pup's character and the potential owner. There is much to be said for this kind of "arranged marriage"; however, for most people, choosing their puppy is an experience they look forward to.

When you view a litter, you may go with the expectation that your puppy will choose you, but it is important not to let your heart rule your head entirely. Remember that the most assertive puppy that comes straight up to you for attention may turn out to be a handful, and not as easy to train as a more polite pup. On the other hand, being drawn out of sympathy to the quiet one who doesn't want to engage with you could be a mistake, especially if you have children, as this puppy may turn out to be defensive and not as friendly.

As a rule of thumb, opting for the middle ground is the safe choice, but whichever puppy catches your eye, there are a number of checks to be made.

Your puppy should be confident and friendly, happy to be handled and inquisitive at your presence. He should be observed playing happily in a clean environment with his littermates. Spend some time with the litter without feeling rushed while you get to know their personalities, then ask

Photo Courtesy of Holly Arrow

the breeder if you can pick up any of those on your short list and look for the following.

The puppy should be clean and dry, smelling of nothing but puppy! His bottom should be clean with no discharge, and his ears and nose should also be clean, with no crustiness or smell. His skin should be clean with no dandruff or sores. His eyes should be clear and bright with no discharge or inflammation. Take a look at his tummy to check there are no hernias, and if he is a boy, check for two descended testicles, although at this stage both may not have dropped, so this is just something to check again before you bring your pup home if he is affected.

When you think you have made your choice, spend a little time with your puppy away from the pack to test your emotional connection with the little character who is going to spend the rest of his life with you.

If your pup has distinctive markings the breeder may have no trouble recognizing him to reserve him for you, but if the pups are all a similar solid color, the breeder may put a colored collar on your pup until the day he is ready to be picked up.

Remember, you are not obliged to choose a puppy just because you have gone to see a litter, and if you have any misgivings about the breeder, the parents, or the puppies themselves, you should walk away and find another litter. It is vitally important that you feel positive about your new dog, as there will be changes and sacrifices in bringing him into your home, and the whole point is that your dog should enrich your life just as you make his complete.

Considerations of a Rescue Dog

It has already been said that Staffordshire Bull Terriers are the most overrepresented breed in dog shelters, and if you are drawn to rescue, you will never have any trouble finding a Staffie in need of a good home.

For most of these dogs, they have been abandoned through no fault of their own. Staffies are overbred, very often indiscriminately, and sometimes from parents with poor temperaments or health issues. They are also a high energy breed, especially when young, and their boisterous nature may prove too much for some owners. Unfortunately, they are also often taken on by people who lack the commitment to train them. This is a great shame as the Staffie is an intelligent and trainable dog, but like any dog, if the training and socialization window in the early months is missed, he will develop antisocial behaviors, and living alongside a human family can become more challenging.

In some cases, a Staffie in rescue can only successfully be rehabilitated by a professional trainer or an owner experienced in the breed. For this reason, when choosing a Staffie from a shelter, you should be guided by the shelter or charity, as they know the temperament of the dog. Furthermore, most dogs taken into rescue will be tested with children, cats, and other household pets, and some will be fostered before rehoming for a more complete evaluation. Any reputable rehoming charity will be committed to matching a dog in their care with the potential owner and home being offered. A successful match is important because when things do not work out, that dog has been let down once again, suffered another blow to his trust, and been set back in his rehabilitation. Also, every organization should offer rescue backup, which means the dog must always be returned to the shelter if the home does not work out at any stage. The dog can never be rehomed independently.

Once you have applied to adopt a dog from a shelter, you will usually be home checked by a representative of the organization, irrespective of your level of experience. This is to make sure that you live where you say you do, and if you rent your property, that you are permitted to keep a dog. It is also to check your family situation, to make sure everyone is committed and understands the implications of adopting a dog, and to check that your home is secure and suitable for a Staffordshire Bull Terrier. It is not an

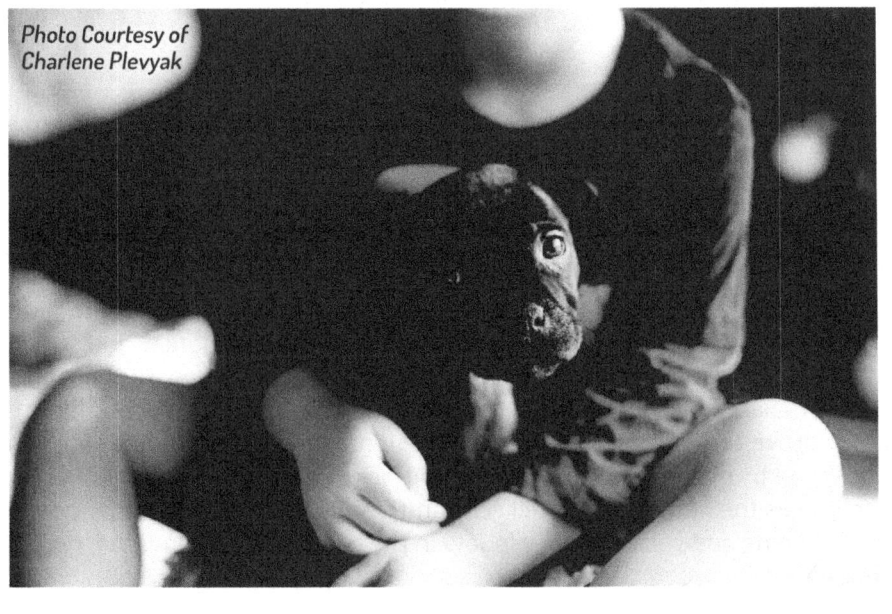

Photo Courtesy of
Charlene Plevyak

exam, and any shortcomings such as a hole in the fence will not fail you; you may just have to attend to anything the home checker notices before you can pick up the dog.

Rehoming a dog is not free. The shelter incurs considerable expense with every dog they take on, so the adoption fee, which may run to several hundred dollars, goes toward these expenses and such things as neutering, vaccinations, parasite treatment, microchipping, and any medical care. The adoption fee also ensures dogs are not seen as a free commodity, to be picked up for dubious purposes such as illegal dog fighting. This is a very real risk for Staffordshire Bull Terriers, as they are generally non-aggressive, so are commonly used as bait dogs. Those who survive this ordeal are often brought into rescue with physical and psychological scars.

If you rescue a Staffordshire Bull Terrier, you will always know you have done a great kindness to an unfortunate dog that has been let down by the species he was born to idolize. You will know this because he will never let you forget it, showering you with the love that is in his nature, and a friendship for life.

CHAPTER 5
Behavioral Issues and Training

"All Staffords should begin at the puppy stage with good solid train-ing. The best Stafford for your home is a trained Stafford. Obedience is a must, and ensure you get the best out of your dog."

Robert Randall
Guardstock Staffordshire Bull Terriers

The Staffordshire Bull Terrier is full of energy and can be headstrong, but they are a very intelligent and trainable breed of dog, and in most instances, firm and consistent application of reward-based training, otherwise known as positive reinforcement, will ensure that your Staffie grows up to be an obedient and loyal part of the family, and a worthy ambassador for a breed that is so often misunderstood.

If you are starting with a puppy, and your pup has been bred from parents with good temperaments, then you are off to a flying start. However, if your dog has not had such a good start in life, he may not have learned how to behave amongst his new human pack, and certain negative behaviors may have become engrained. This chapter gives a few tips about training your dog to fit into home life. It is usually perfectly possible to train your dog yourself, though puppy classes are a great help with socialization, expert guidance, and moral support. If your dog is more challenging, you should never feel you have failed if you call in a professional behaviorist. Quite often their experience will soon help you set your dog onto the correct path. Every caring owner wants to do the best for their Staffordshire Bull Terrier, and helping him learn acceptable behavior is the greatest favor you can do for your dog, ensuring he will never become another statistic in animal rescue.

HELPFUL TIP
Exercise

Staffordshire Bull Terriers have a lot of energy and need plenty of exercise. Many behavioral issues can be tied to a lack of exercise, so plan on lots of long walks or jogs on a leash or running around the backyard to help reduce behavioral problems.

Photo Courtesy of
Jason Lee

Housebreaking

Housebreaking is the first thing you will need to teach your dog if you have just brought home a ten-week-old puppy. However, if you have adopted an older dog, there is a chance you may also have to teach him to toilet outside, especially if he has been kenneled previously and never lived in a family home. Retraining an older dog can be more of a challenge as you are having to overcome engrained behavior, but an adult dog does at least have physical control over his bladder and bowels, which a young puppy is still in the process of developing.

Whichever of these situations you find yourself in, you need to capitalize on the fact that all dogs have an innate instinct to keep their sleeping area clean. If a dog regularly soils his bed, he should see a vet, as he may have a physical problem. Even confined in a kennel or crate, a dog will do his business at the other end. This is one reason why, if you are crate-training your puppy, you should not get too large a crate, as he needs to see all of it as his bed, and hold his bladder and bowels until you let him out in the yard. Needless to say, this should be at frequent intervals while he is young

Photo Courtesy of
Brooke Downey

and his control is not fully developed. Otherwise he will accidentally soil his bed, which will cause him distress and set back his training.

If you are not crate training, you still need to let your puppy out into the yard very frequently, to preempt any accidents indoors. Setting a regular routine will help, and always let your puppy out on waking, after eating, and before bed. When your dog is outside, you should simply observe him and recognize when he is about to do his business. Not every male puppy will cock a leg in the early months, so as with a female, look for an intention to squat, and then use your command word, "busy" or "pee-pees" or whatever word you wish to use. You then have every excuse to praise your dog profusely for doing the right thing, and he will soon learn to associate the word with the action, and relieve himself on command, which is extremely useful when you wish your dog to be comfortable before you go out, or last thing in the evening.

If your dog has an accident in the house, which is inevitable, you should never make a fuss, unless you catch your dog in the act, in which case you should whisk him outdoors to make the point that the yard is the place to toilet. Reprimanding your dog when you find a wet patch on the carpet will just confuse him, as he will not make the association if he did this a while ago. You may even make him stress-incontinent if you punish him for accidentally toileting indoors, which is counterproductive. You should just clean the area thoroughly with an ammonia-neutralizing product or a carpet shampooer if you have one, to ensure the dog is not drawn back by the smell to soil the same area.

If you have a male dog, you may find you have to contend with scent marking in the home, which is extremely unpleasant and unhygienic. Castrating your dog will usually eliminate or reduce this behavior.

If you have an adult dog that has been previously housebroken, but suddenly starts to soil the house, you should consider two possibilities. Has there been something unsettling for the dog that is causing a stress reaction? Or does the dog have a physical problem, such as a bladder infection, or in the case of a spayed female, a slackening of the urinary sphincter, as discussed in Chapter 12? Both of these conditions require veterinary attention but are usually easily treated.

Photo Courtesy of
Jashvir Singh

Chewing and Destructive Behavior

"Staffords are 'mouthy' be prepared to teach your dog proper eti-
quette about chewing and biting your heals. They are incredible smart
and will learn quickly not to do this, but that is up to you to train this."

Teri Keetch
Dyna Staffs

If your Staffordshire Bull Terrier is a puppy, chewing is a completely natural behavior for him. It is a part of exploring his new world, and it also relieves the discomfort of teething. Between the age of three and six months, your puppy will gradually lose all his 28 baby teeth, and these will be replaced by 42 adult teeth. This is when there are extra teeth pushing through the gums, as well as larger teeth replacing those in the baby sockets. It is hardly surprising your Staffie pup is constantly aware of his mouth over this period, and will chew indiscriminately. As his owner, the trick to staying one step ahead of the game is to take away as many objects as possible that you do not wish him to chew, and replace them with objects he can chew safely. Some suggestions are given in chapter 10 about dental health, but popular choices are deer's antlers (which will not splinter like bones), a Nylabone® (tough nylon chew), and a rubber Kong®, which can also occupy your dog by being filled with a tasty treat like pâté, xylitol-free peanut butter, or some of his daily kibble ration.

Older dogs that still like to chew can be given a commercial dental chew, a dried pig's ear, various dried offal products, or a fresh bone (never cooked). However, do supervise your dog with chews that break down, in case a part of any of these should splinter or lodge in the gullet.

If you catch your dog chewing something he shouldn't, such as your shoe, you should remove it with a firm "no," but always replace it with an approved chew. This is because chewing is not a bad behavior, it is natural. However, your dog needs to learn what is appropriate to chew, and what he must leave alone.

Unfortunately, Staffordshire Bull Terriers can be prone to destructive behavior as they are high energy and easily bored. If you are very house proud, the Staffie may not be the breed for you, or you may consider a "trash room" for your dog, where you do not keep any valued things. However, if your dog is only destructive in your absence, despite being left with safe chews and toys, this may be a sign of separation anxiety, which is discussed next.

Separation Anxiety

Your Staffie was not born to be alone. He was raised by his mom in a pack with his siblings, and when you came along, you filled that newly made void in his life, and became his world. It is natural that he doesn't want you to leave his side. However, life doesn't work like that, and sometimes your dog will need to be left alone in the home. Whether or not your dog copes easily with this has much to do with his temperament. However, you can teach him to feel calm and settled when you are not there, by giving him the confidence that you will always come back.

If you are crate training your puppy, you are at an advantage, because when you are out of the home, you know your dog is not destroying the house; the most damage he can do is to his bed. But you don't want him to even feel stressed enough to tear up his bed, so you must begin teaching him to be left alone by just leaving him for a very short time, initially just a few minutes.

Always make sure your dog is comfortable before you leave him and has been outside to do his business. You can leave him with a safe, indestructible chew to distract him, and some owners like to leave the radio or television on to mask outside noises.

Do not make a fuss when you leave your dog. You should ignore him on your exit, and on your return. Otherwise he thinks being left is a big deal, but by downplaying it, you tell him it's nothing to worry about. If you hear your dog whining, don't come back through the door until he is quiet. Then return quietly through the door and let your dog out into the yard. Once he is calm, you can give him a pat and tell him he is a good boy.

Build up the time you leave your dog in gradual increments. You should not leave a young puppy for more than a couple of hours as he will need to toilet, and soiling indoors will set back his training. An adult dog should not be left for more than four hours. If you need to be out for longer than that, you should employ someone to come in and let your dog out for a comfort break.

If you live somewhere where the weather is favorable enough for your dog to live in the yard while you are out, and your yard is secure, you may eventually be able to leave your dog for longer as he is free to toilet as he needs. However, your bond is not helped by leaving him for long periods; he still needs company.

If you have adopted a dog with severe separation anxiety, this should have been flagged up by the rescue, as severely affected dogs may need someone around all the time and cannot be homed where the owner is out at work during the day. The Staffie is a breed that much prefers human company to that of other dogs, but if your Staffie is sociable and 100% non-aggressive with other dogs, you might consider getting him another non-dominant companion, but ideally not two males. If problems persist, it is worth consulting a professional behaviorist to look at your individual situation and use their experience to advise how you can best help your dog.

Building your dog's trust is all a part of making him a settled and happy dog, and this is a gradual process. Remain consistent, and your dog will learn what is expected of him, and that you will never let him down.

Recall

One of the strongest attributes of the Staffordshire Bull Terrier working in your favor when recall training is the fact that your Staffie just loves humans, so being with you is his best thing, and unlike many other breeds, escape just isn't on his radar!

Having said that, being outside is exciting for your dog. There are lots of new sights and smells, and if you are in a park there may be other dogs and people. Staffies are full of energy and readily stimulated, so in view of these challenges, you need to ensure that you are even more exciting to be around than the other things competing for your dog's attention. An upbeat and excitable voice is a must, and some tasty treats in your pocket will help too. However, you are outside so that your dog can enjoy himself and explore his surroundings too, so you need to be able to give your dog permission to leave your side, and to be able to call him back reliably as well.

Giving your dog the "free" command as you send him away puts you in control of his free movement, so that you do not fully lose his attention and can call your dog back more readily. In the training stages, you should recall your dog frequently, and reward him when he returns to your side with a treat or praise. Also, don't walk in a straight line, but keep changing direction, to make your dog keep his focus on you. Taking a ball out with you can help keep your dog's attention on you, as Staffies love to play. However, you shouldn't play ball or overexert a young puppy, as his joints and bones are still soft.

If your dog runs off, never chastise him on his return, or he will associate coming back with being told off. Early recall training should take place in a safe, enclosed environment like a securely fenced yard, field, or park, and away from traffic and other dogs. If your dog proves more challenging, you can consider a long training line attached to a harness (never a collar), to help your dog learn to respect his range. These long lines are best used away from other people as they can cause entanglement.

Teaching your dog good recall is a high priority with the Staffordshire Bull Terrier, especially if you plan to walk him in public areas, as many people, especially children and some parents, are wary of the breed, however unfairly. Also, Staffies can be reactive with other dogs, which is discussed in Chapter 7. Being able to control your dog is the best way to show the world that Staffies do not deserve their reputation, as well as ensuring everybody can enjoy their time outside.

Car Chasing

Not every breed of dog will chase cars, but this dangerous behavior is often seen in Staffies, as they are so energetic and drawn to moving objects. It goes without saying that no dog should be off leash near traffic unless he is completely bomb proof. But some dogs may be loose in their own front yard when a car comes by, and they will be drawn to chase it. The obvious answer is always to keep your dog behind a secure fence. However, as we are all fallible, and your dog may sometimes find himself off leash when a car passes by, if he is prone to this behavior, he needs to learn the "leave" command.

You can prepare for this by putting your dog on a leash and throwing a toy for him. His instinct is to go for the toy, but immediately after you have thrown it, you say firmly "leave," and keep the leash tight. Treat and praise your dog for staying by your side. You are thus teaching your dog to override his chase instinct.

HELPFUL TIP

Be the Boss

The Staffordshire Bull Terrier needs an owner that is confident in themselves and their training ability. The Staffy isn't a good choice for people who like to sit back and let their dog do its own thing because a Staffy will take full advantage of it and can cause a wide variety of problems from chewing up your furniture to chasing cats to killing other dogs.

Build this up to having a friend run past or ride by on a bike, as car chasers are usually drawn to chase joggers and cyclists too. Tell your dog to "leave," and restrain him with the leash, although giving him some slack allows him to make the choice of his own volition at this stage. Reward him for good behavior, and keep practicing until he is reliable 100% of the time.

Digging

Digging is part of any dog's DNA, but unfortunately the Staffordshire Bull Terrier can be a very determined digger, owing to his high energy levels and low boredom threshold. The Staffie is also a strong and muscular dog, so in a short space of time, he can make a large hole, and if he chooses to make this under your yard fence, he will soon have an escape route if he is outside unsupervised.

There are four approaches to controlling digging behavior in your Staffordshire Bull Terrier, and these are supervision, redirection, distraction, and prevention.

As you cannot deprogram your dog's instinct to dig, you need to outsmart him by diverting his digging behavior to an acceptable area and not under your fence or in your flower border. Choose a spot and either dig it over to break the surface, or add sand to make a sand pit, or bury some things he will enjoy finding. Now supervise your dog, and when you catch him digging elsewhere, whisk him to his designated digging area. Hopefully he will find digging in this spot far more rewarding, and in time will understand the difference between acceptable and unacceptable places to exercise his urge to dig.

Staffies like to dig as it relieves boredom, but also because his primal instincts tell him buried food keeps longer and is safe from other predators. For this reason, a dog that digs should not be given bones unsupervised as he will instinctively want to bury them. However, if you bury a bone in his designated digging area it can be very rewarding for him, as long as you supervise to ensure he does not go off to re-bury it elsewhere.

You can distract your dog from digging out of boredom by providing alternative entertainment, such as activity toys like a Kong® stuffed with something tasty, or a safe chew. Don't leave him with a ball, as he will obviously want to bury it!

To prevent your dog from digging in unacceptable places, you may need to consider burying your fence panels one or two feet into the ground, but another approach is to lay chicken wire or half-buried rocks along the base of your fence as this will act as a deterrent. There are products on the market aimed to deter dogs from digging in a favored spot, but other low-tech deterrents include chili sauce or even buried dog poo. However, there is no accounting for the dog that actually likes the taste of these things!

As with all training, the key is to keep it positive and consistent. Do not punish your dog for a natural dog behavior, and try to anticipate how his mind works to stay one step ahead of him!

Biting

Photo Courtesy of Helen Nolan

Like chewing, biting is a natural behavior for a puppy, but it is vitally important that your puppy learns bite inhibition during his early training, as a dog that has missed out on this lesson may go on to use biting as a defensive action. Not only can this cause injury, but it does nothing to rehabilitate the reputation of the Staffordshire Bull Terrier.

If you are fortunate enough to be starting from scratch with a puppy, you will find he wants to mouth your hands the whole time, and sometimes he may nip. When playing with his littermates, puppies will squeal loudly when nipped by another, and this signifies they have overstepped the mark. You need to do the same. Also, you should reinforce the point by depriving your pup of what he wants, your attention. Turn your back on your puppy when he nips you, then return to play when he settles down.

Also, to train a dog out of mouthing behavior, you can hold a treat in your clenched hand without releasing it while he mouths your hand, then only open your hand when your dog takes his nose away. He will learn that he does not get what he wants by mouthing your hand.

This behavior should not be apparent in an adult dog, but some dogs who have not learned bite inhibition as puppies may demonstrate aggressive biting, which is a serious behavioral issue. It may even lead to destruction of the dog, so it needs to be addressed.

Dogs that bite out of fear or aggression usually show warning signs, such as rigidity or a drawing back of the lips, but children might not recognize these signs to back off. A behaviorist should be sought if your dog demonstrates aggressive biting, and he should always be muzzled in public.

Coprophagy

Coprophagy, also known as coprophagia, is a particularly gross habit common among Staffies, as well as some other breeds. It means they will eat their own feces, or that of other dogs, cats, or wildlife. Unfortunately, no scientific study has yet found the definitive answer for this revolting behavior, though theories range from dietary deficiencies, to a primal instinct to clean up, to rebalancing their microbiome, to simple greed and the acquisition of a gross appetite. And since we do not understand the reason for coprophagy, we cannot prevent it, therefore we have to manage it.

The answer, if your dog likes to eat poop, is to ensure as far as possible that he does not have access to it. This means keeping the yard clean and being vigilant when out on a walk, especially if your dog is allowed off leash.

If your dog enjoys poop on a regular basis, then he is likely to have a greater intestinal parasite burden than the average Staffordshire Bull Terrier. He should therefore be wormed with a tapeworming tablet every three months as well as receiving a monthly treatment for roundworms and other ascarids.

The types of behavioral issues you will encounter in your journey with your Staffie may range from managing his natural instincts, to unacceptable issues that may only be addressed with professional help. You will also find a wide range of advice strategies offered to you by friends, books, TV, and online, so if one method fails, there will always be other approaches to try. Positive reinforcement is the key, as well as consistent and firm application, with a strong-minded Staffie. There is nothing more rewarding than the pride you can feel in a well-behaved Staffordshire Bull Terrier.

CHAPTER 6
Obedience Training

"Staffords are highly intelligent and easy to train. They are eager to please and get their feeling hurt easily if they feel they disappointed you. Consistency in your words and praise is all they need to catch on quickly to what their person expects from them."

Teri Keetch
Dyna Staffs

The Staffordshire Bull Terrier can be an obstinate breed; however, Staffies are very intelligent and they think they are human, so with firm and consistent training they can become highly obedient. There is something very satisfying in owning an obedient Staffie, as you know that your dog is helping to dismantle the breed's unfair reputation every time he meets a new person. An obedient dog is also less of a danger to others or to himself, and better able to live harmoniously in the family home. So, putting in the training at an early stage is the best favor you can do for your new Staffie puppy, as the vital training window is in the first six months before adolescence. Enrolling your pup for socialization classes as soon as he has completed his first course of vaccinations will lead on to obedience classes, and whether or not you have had dogs before, it can help to have the moral support of other owners and expert advice on hand in training your Staffie puppy. It's also more fun and sets a routine that is easier to stick to.

If you have adopted an older dog that has not been fortunate enough to receive early obedience training, you may find the job more challenging. However, obedience classes are not only for puppies. As long as your dog is vaccinated and not aggressive, he will be welcome to join a class. Alternatively, if you are struggling with his training, you may consider individual sessions with a behaviorist. However disobedient your dog may be when you first adopt him, there will be techniques you can use to improve his obedience, and a behaviorist will be able to identify what motivates your individual dog.

The harsh and sometimes cruel methods of obedience training used in the past have fallen out of favor in recent times, because they do not create a bond of trust between owner and dog. Today, dogs are taught using positive reinforcement methods, which rewards a dog for a correct response.

Positive reinforcement generally uses a treat to reward correct behavior, and this may be a tiny piece of something irresistible such as sausage, or a small training treat from your pet store, or homemade dried liver chips. Just make sure you adjust your dog's daily food ration accordingly. Some dogs that are not motivated by food may actually respond better to a favorite toy. Some classes also use a clicker to reinforce correct behavior, which can eventually be used without the treat. Just like "Pavlov's Dog," positive reinforcement uses "associative conditioning," so with constant repetition, the dog knows exactly what to do on command by associating word and action.

There are many different approaches to obedience training, and the following sections just give one example for teaching the basic commands. If you have been taught a different way in classes, then as long as this is working, and it follows the positive reinforcement method, you should stick to it, as your dog appreciates consistency to avoid confusion.

Photo Courtesy of
Lucy Brazier

How to Teach Sit

HELPFUL TIP
Training isn't Optional

All dogs need obedience training, but it's arguably more important for bully breeds like the Staffordshire Bull Terrier than other dogs. This is only partly due to the chance that they could become aggressive. The best reason to make sure your Staffy is well-trained is due to the public perception that bully-breed dogs are vicious. A friendly, obedient Staffordshire Bull Terrier is a good ambassador for all bully breeds.

As a preliminary to teaching "Sit," you should first teach your dog the "Look at me" command, because without your dog's full attention you are fighting a losing battle, and Staffies are easily distracted.

Most Staffies are motivated by tasty treats, especially if you have something particularly delicious in your closed hand. Do not reward your dog for pawing at your hand, but when he is making eye contact alone, you should promptly say "Look at me," and give your dog the treat.

Initially, you should not use any new command to prompt an action, but only when the dog is actively doing the action you require. This is because he needs to associate the word with the correct action. As you repeat the exercise and your dog gets better at it, you can separate the command from the action by saying "Look at me" as a prompt to your dog to be still and make eye contact.

So, once you have your dog's attention, and he now knows he can earn treats by doing what you are requiring him to do, show him the treat in your hand by bringing it to his nose, and then raise your hand. Your dog's nose will follow the treat, and his hind quarters will instinctively lower.

You have created the "Sit" position in your dog without him being consciously aware of it, so you now need to associate the word "Sit" with the action. So only as your dog's hind quarters begin to lower should you use the word "Sit." Treat your dog, allow him to stand, and repeat the process many times.

As long as your dog remains focused, you can then separate the word from the action to make it a conscious prompt by telling your dog to "Sit" while he is still in the stand position.

It is very important to end the session on a positive note with a correct response, and to keep training sessions short, because once your dog loses focus, it will set the learning process back. Little and often is key to success.

Photo Courtesy of
Lucy Whitmore

How to Teach Stay

Once your Staffie knows how to sit on command, he needs to learn that he is still under your control, and not allowed to get up unless you allow him. This can be a challenge for a boisterous Staffordshire Bull Terrier. So do not expect too much from him too soon, as the length of time you can expect him to stay will need to be built up incrementally.

Alongside the word "Stay," you need to teach the command "Free" to release your dog from the stay. When you first get your dog to sit, you still have his full attention, as he is expecting a treat. Therefore, you need to delay the treat for just a few seconds, and as he is quiet and expectant, use the command word "Stay," because he is actively staying.

As you give your dog the treat, he is likely to get up, so you need to associate this release with the word "Free," and as you give the treat and say "Free," you should lead the dog away from the spot with a semi-circular sweep of your hand, then allow him the treat. This way, you are taking any decisions away from your dog and remaining the controller of his actions, which is important in your dog's mind as he needs to learn to always defer to your commands to be an obedient dog.

Repeat the process several times to reinforce it, gradually extending the length of time you can keep your dog's attention in "Stay." As previously, do not extend the session beyond your dog's concentration span, and always end on a positive note.

Photo Courtesy of
Daniel Pickering
Photo by Diamond Dogs Fine Art Pet Photography

How to Teach Lie Down

Teaching "Lie down" adopts the same principle as teaching "Sit." That is to say, you encourage your dog into the correct body position by the way you use the treat to guide his action.

Now that your dog also understands "Stay" and does not simply get up as soon as he has sat for you, he is ready to learn to lie down, which always impresses your visitors and shows them a Staffie on his best behavior.

With your dog in the "Sit," tell your dog to "Stay" so that his attention is still fully on you in anticipation of the reward. You should

Photo Courtesy of Megan Murray

then bring your hand containing the treat to the floor between your dog's front legs. His head and neck will follow your hand, whereby you bring the treat along the floor toward yourself. As you do this, your dog's forelegs will creep along the floor following the treat and instinctively he will lower his shoulders to the floor, creating the "Lie down" position. As his elbows reach the floor, use the command "Lie down" and treat your dog. You can now release him with the "Free" command.

Another technique, if you find that your dog's hind quarters go up as his front legs go down, is to use your free arm like a limbo pole across his back, and continue to draw the treat toward you. As his body creeps toward the treat, he will be forced to lower his hind quarters under your arm.

Continue with as many repetitions as your dog's concentration span will allow, and practice every day to drive the message home.

How to Teach Walk on the Leash

Photo Courtesy of Rhian Evans

Staffordshire Bull Terriers are only medium size, but they are very energetic, strong, and muscular. Therefore, if they are not taught to walk nicely on a loose leash, they are very capable of pulling their handler over, or dragging them down the road. This is unsafe and unacceptable, so training your dog to walk on the leash is a high priority.

If you have a young puppy, you may find yourself with a ball of uncontrolled energy at the end of a leash, and your mission will be to tame your dog and get him to focus on you.

If you have adopted an older dog that has not been taught to walk on the leash, you may feel you are having to restrain him and it can be a real physical battle. An adult dog is a lot stronger than a puppy. You may find practicing in an indoor environment, such as training classes, helps your dog to focus as he has less to pull for without a horizon in his sights. Dogs can behave very differently indoors to out and it is helpful to start off where you are more likely to succeed. But you shouldn't be discouraged once you move into an outdoor environment if your dog is immediately a hooligan again. Just continue patiently with the same techniques, as Staffies are very capable learners.

When training a dog to walk on the leash, the leash is usually attached to the collar, as the dog is more sensitive to contact. The exception would be if your dog pulls to the extent that he could damage the bones of his neck, in which case a harness is preferable. Control harnesses are a last resort if your basic training fails, but it is worth consulting a professional for help before resorting to a gadget to enforce leash-training. Choke chains should never be used as they can cause injury.

Once again, getting your dog's attention is the first step to teaching him to walk on a loose leash. With your leash in your right hand, position your dog to your left, then take a few steps forward. If he rushes ahead, you should stop. When the leash is loose again, take a few more steps. If your dog walks nicely, even momentarily, slip him a treat from your left hand (it helps to keep these handy in a pocket or fanny pack). Always stop when your dog pulls on the leash. He needs to learn he will not get to where he thinks he is going by pulling. You are unlikely to make any progress that could count as a walk, but it is important to accept this is training and not recreation.

Once your dog has improved at paying attention and can walk more than a few paces on a loose leash, step it up by changing your direction frequently, keeping your dog focused and interested by being upbeat about how well he is doing! Staffies are excitable, so don't overexcite your dog so much that he starts jumping up, and only slip him his treats when he is walking very nicely by your side.

If you have been practicing indoors or in your back yard and your dog has progressed well, you can now repeat the exercises in a wider outdoor environment. It is worth choosing an area without too many distractions, so go for somewhere without other people and dogs to start off with. Eventually you can graduate to the park and to busy urban environments, and wean your dog off the treat reward. Every new step may set your dog back as he deals with more space and distractions, but overall, he will be consolidating his progress.

This chapter has given a few suggestions for starting basic obedience training, but just as there are many different approaches, so are there many different Staffordshire Bull Terriers out there with a diversity of temperaments. It is important to stick with a training approach for long enough to give your dog a chance, but if it really isn't working, another technique may be more successful with your dog.

If you are struggling, it is worth consulting a professional for advice. And if you have adopted your dog from a rescue center, they may have a behaviorist of their own who can help you for no extra cost.

It is worth bearing in mind that a previously well-trained dog may regress during adolescence from 6-12 months of age, and you should not lose heart, but simply keep up the training, taking a step back and returning to basics if necessary.

In general, though, consistent and patient reward-based training, along with a healthy dose of firmness, will earn your Staffie's respect without compromising his affection. And while he may never join the circus, he will make you proud by learning basic obedience skills to make both your lives that much easier and safer.

HELPFUL TIP
Leash Training

Staffordshire Bull Terriers are much stronger than you would expect for their small size. Training them to heel on a leash is critical, both for you to enjoy walks and to keep your Staffy away from trouble rather than letting him drag you into a bad situation.

CHAPTER 7
Socialization

The best thing you can do is to socialize your Stafford. Let them play with children and friends, but be sure supervision. Let them be around other animals, but introduce them slowly. MAKE SURE your puppy has had all their vaccinations and has been wormed."

Robert Randall
Guardstock Staffordshire Bull Terriers

Despite the Staffordshire Bull Terrier's reputation as an intimidating dog, most Staffies are non-aggressive and very affectionate toward their family. Although it is impossible to make generalizations with the breed, on the whole, Staffies prefer humans to other dogs. For this reason, socializing a Staffie with people is usually very straightforward, but problems can sometimes arise when socializing a Staffordshire Bull Terrier with his own species.

Photo Courtesy of
Helen Nolan

Photo Courtesy of Lauren Ford

Importance of Socialization

The other problem with the public perception of the Staffordshire Bull Terrier is that the breed will be given considerably less slack than other breeds if he shows any sign of aggression at all, especially if he should attack a person or another dog. Because of the association with the Pit Bull Terrier, people will immediately label the dog as "to type." At best, this further tarnishes the unfair reputation of the breed, and at worse, your Staffie may be taken for assessment for an offense that a Yorkshire Terrier would have gotten away with. In the ongoing battle to redress the Staffie's reputation, every owner should strive to create a breed ambassador in their dog. Not only will this help to overcome public prejudice, but a well-socialized dog will never find himself in a situation where he might be destroyed for an act of aggression, not to mention the damage he could do to another person or dog.

When to Socialize Your New Dog

It is never too early to socialize your Staffie. Your dog has in fact been socialized from birth by interaction with his littermates, and a good breeder will also ensure he has got well used to being handled too. So, when you pick up your three-month-old puppy, he is off to a flying start. Your job is to continue his socialization training after he has been removed from his mother and his littermates, because at this point, he is suddenly on his own. His new family are human, and in bonding with you he forgets he is a dog!

Photo Courtesy of
Bethany Hughes

Introducing Your New Staffordshire Bull Terrier to Other Dogs

"Staffords don't tend to like to cause conflict, but they won't back down once it is started. Starting socialization young is the key here, and stopping problems before they escalate is very important. Don't ever let a strange dog approach your Stafford without being prepared. It should be done slowly and cautiously."

Teri Keetch
Dyna Staffs

As soon as your puppy has completed his first course of vaccinations, he is ready to make new friends of his own kind. You can find out about puppy socialization classes in your area by asking at your veterinary surgery. Classes, or puppy play groups, create an ideal, safe environment for your new Staffie puppy to interact with other dogs, as all will be at the same life stage, with the same puppy body language. It is a non-threatening way for your dog to learn to feel comfortable around dogs of other breeds, before any have developed fear or aggression through bad life experiences.

Your puppy will also need to learn how to socialize with adult dogs, as up to now, he may never have encountered another adult dog apart from his mother. Adult dogs use a totally different language, and may have low tolerance for a bad-mannered, exuberant puppy. So do pick his playmates carefully as it is very important that your puppy doesn't have any bad experiences at this formative stage. Meeting a friend with a docile, friendly dog in neutral territory such as a quiet park is a good choice. Otherwise, it is better to invite your friend and their dog to your yard rather than theirs, as your puppy is not yet territorial, whereas the other dog may be more defensive in his own home until they get to know each other.

If you already have a dog, and are bringing your new Staffie home for the first time, it is advisable not to bring the new dog through the front door straight into a confined space for the first meeting, as this creates a confrontational dynamic. There are two schools of thought with first greetings. One is that you take both dogs straight out into the yard where they have plenty of space to get acquainted, and the dogs can back off when things get heated. The other approach is to take the resident dog into the yard or out for a walk, while the new dog makes himself at home indoors. Then the resident dog can go into the house and find the new dog, which is a gentler introduction than throwing the pair together at the front door.

When you introduce another dog into a home where there is already a dog in residence, it is perfectly normal for there to be a period of adjustment, and scraps may occur while the dogs are sorting out the pecking order. It is useful to have a crate for the puppy, especially if the resident dog is elderly, as sometimes time-out is needed. The dogs will gradually learn to bond, especially when taken out for walks together in neutral territory. If problems persist, you may consider consulting a behaviorist, or if you have adopted a rescue dog, the rescue organization should be able to offer expert advice, as they will be very familiar with integration issues. They are also invested in making the adoption work out.

Introducing Your New Staffordshire Bull Terrier to Children

The Staffordshire Bull Terrier is commonly known as the "Nanny Dog" because of his devotion to the children in the family, and this reflects his true instinct to protect and befriend children, far from his negative reputation.

Having said that, children often unwittingly provoke a reaction in a dog, however tolerant, by being disrespectful of his space, teasing, or hurting the dog. So rather than training the dog, the right way to socialize your Staffordshire Bull Terrier with children is to train the children!

If your child is a very young toddler, you should expect to supervise your child at all times with your Staffie, but it is never too early to start teaching your child to be gentle and to treat their four-legged friend with respect. Your child should learn never to pull your dog's ears, poke his eyes, pull his tail or ride him like a pony. Show your child how to approach your dog quietly from the side so that your dog can see them, then gently stroke the dog at the back of his head and neck, and talk quietly to the dog.

An older child may be ready to learn about body language, which is important if they are to be left unsupervised with the dog. You should teach your child that when a dog stiffens its body, backs away, or draws back his lips, he should immediately be left alone. And make sure your child understands they shouldn't touch the dog while he is eating or sleeping.

Some dogs may feel they belong higher up in the family hierarchy than the children, and this can sometimes make them challenge the children. This is unusual for a Staffie because they love children so much; however, to prevent it from happening, households with children should ensure the dog sleeps in his own bed, not on the parents' bed, and the children should help look after the dog, giving him his food and being involved with his walks.

Reactive Dogs

If you have adopted a dog from a rescue center, it is the highest duty of the rescue to ensure that the dog is not reactive with children before placing it in a family home. Sometimes a rescue dog will have had a prior bad experience with children who have treated him with disrespect, and that may have led to the dog becoming reactive. It is highly irresponsible to place a dog that is reactive with children into a family home, as safety is far more important than rehabilitation, and no child should be put in a position of danger. Therefore, a dog that is reactive with children should be returned to the rescue for placement in a more suitable home.

A more common situation with the breed is for a Staffordshire Bull Terrier to be reactive with other dogs. Unless a Staffie has been brought up around other dogs through purposeful socialization, or in a multi-dog household, he will be inclined to see himself as human, and be unwilling to share his owner's attentions with any other presumptuous dog encroaching on his space. He may also feel he has to protect his owner from attack.

Many Staffies find themselves in rescue because of such behavioral issues that have arisen through lack of early training. So, if you have bought a puppy from well-researched bloodlines, and you are socializing him daily with other dogs, you are very unlikely to end up with a reactive dog. However, if you have taken on a rescue Staffie who has had a poor start, you may find you are dealing with aggression toward other dogs. It is worth noting that male dogs generally are more reactive with other male dogs than with female dogs.

Rather than avoid all interaction with other dogs, which is not only restrictive, but will never address your dog's issues, the key to rehabilitating a reactive dog is through gradual habituation. This means controlled exposure to the trigger until the dog no longer sees it as a threat.

As with all training, this should begin in a controlled environment with the help of another friend with a non-reactive dog. However, although you need control over your dog, you should not restrain him on a short leash as the tension will cause him discomfort. Rather you need to create an atmosphere of calm so he feels relaxed, so you need a harness and long line (about 15 feet in length, looped around your arm). Take your dog into the open on a loose line, but keep his attention by being fun, while encouraging him to sniff and explore. As your friend approaches with their dog, do not guide your dog toward the other dog, but keep his movement natural and allow him to go where he wishes.

There will come a point when your dog notices the other dog, and may become rigid or take up the slack on the line. At this point you can use positive distraction by hand-feeding lots of small, tasty treats, or scattering them on the ground for your dog to snuffle up rather than being stressed about the other dog. Or if your dog prefers a toy to treats, you can use this to distract him. Make sure you have switched your dog's attention onto you rather than the "threat." If necessary, you can stand between your dog and the other dog and use the "Look at me" command, treating for a correct response.

You should only treat your dog in the presence of the trigger, so that he begins to associate what he perceived as something negative into something that is actually positive, as it produces treats or a toy. Clicker training is very useful to reinforce correct choices in your dog's mind.

It is important to understand that results will not happen overnight, and only through regular repetition will you reprogram your dog's mind. As you progress, you can increase the level of challenge by going into more public places with more unknown dogs. But if your dog is at all unpredictable, he should always be muzzled in public places to ensure no other dog gets hurt.

When Socialization Goes Bad

Unfortunately, sometimes during the socialization process, things may go wrong. This commonly occurs when an unknown dog gets too close, provoking a reaction. It is normal for dogs to be off-leash, enjoying free exercise in public spaces, and it is also normal for dogs to run up to other dogs to greet them. Usually a bit of dog language occurs at this point, with sniffing at both ends, tail wagging, and maybe a game of chase. But sometimes one of the dogs feels threatened. They will usually stiffen their body and draw back their lips. They may snarl, and the other dog instinctively knows to back off. A confrontation has been averted. Bear in mind, though, that a puppy does not yet know how to read the signs, and can be intensely annoying to an adult dog, so always supervise introductions carefully with a puppy. Also, sometimes a dog may snap without prior warning, even launching a full attack. If your Staffie is on the receiving end, then this may significantly set back his socialization.

There are some things you can do to prevent this situation from occurring in the first place. When walking your dog, you should always remain vigilant for the presence of other dogs, so that they do not seem to appear from nowhere, startling your dog. You should also note their body language as you see them approach, and calmly change direction with your dog if you see any reactive warning signs in either dog. Keep a toy or ball on hand, or some training treats, to divert your dog's attention.

If your dog is on the leash, be aware he may feel more threatened by the approach of an unknown dog because he cannot get away. The same applies for the other dog if it is yours that is free and the other is on the leash. Uncontrolled introductions should not take place in this unequal situation.

If both your dog and the other dog are on the leash, it is worth remembering the three-second rule. If the two dogs come face-to-face, go rigid, and stare each other out for three seconds, it is time to walk your dog promptly away before the situation turns bad.

If your dog has been attacked, you will probably need to go back to basics with socialization. Invite some calm playmates over for a positive experience, then arrange some quiet walks with dogs that your dog knows. Build his confidence up again slowly, but don't avoid other dogs, as that will create a lasting problem.

If your dog has been the aggressor, this is a wake-up call that you are moving too quickly with his training. Also, that he must be muzzled. Muzzling a dog alone will help ensure other dog owners do not allow a free approach from their dog, so it may not only prevent confrontation, but will ensure no injury occurs if it does. Dogs that continue to be reactive may wear a yellow vest, harness, or bandana with the message "I need space" or "Reactive Dog" to encourage the cooperation of other dog owners.

Most Staffies will grow up to interact very positively, both with people and other dogs, and there is nothing more life-affirming than the sight of a huge Staffie smile as your dog enjoys playing in the park. However, social confidence needs to be built up from an early age so should never be left to chance. But if you have adopted a fearful older dog, there will usually be strategies you can put in place to help him build his trust and overcome reactive issues. Helping a damaged dog to enjoy life again is one of the greatest gifts you can give a Staffordshire Bull Terrier.

CHAPTER 8
Traveling

Preparations for Travel

Some dogs are excellent at traveling, while others find the whole process very stressful, leading to their owners feeling anxious and overwhelmed. The category your dog will fall into is not usually breed-specific, but rather each dog is an individual. Therefore, you may have a Staffie which is an excellent traveler, or you may have one which gets nervous. Making the appropriate preparations for travel will ensure that the whole journey goes as smoothly as possible, regardless of how your dog is feeling.

The first step to take before you go on a long journey is to check with your vet that your dog is fit to travel. Your vet will be able to give your Staffie a full clinical examination to look for any reason that he shouldn't travel, such as illnesses which affect the respiratory system. He will also be able to give you tips for travel if your Staffie has certain ailments. For example, if your dog has arthritis, which we talk about further in Chapter 14, he may need more frequent stops to keep him mobile and ensure he doesn't seize up.

At the vet appointment you can also ensure your Staffie's microchip is working, or have one put in if it isn't. A microchip is a small piece of metal about the size of a grain of rice, inserted in between the shoulder blades. It contains a unique number when scanned, which is linked to all your contact details at the microchip company. That way, should your dog run away or get lost, he can easily be reunited with you. This obviously only works if your details are kept updated with the microchip company, so if you ever move house or change cell number, ensure that you contact them to change these.

Finally, while at the vet's, it is a good opportunity to pick up any chronic medications which

HELPFUL TIP
Breed Restrictions

As you may know, many places have breed restrictions in place. These breed restrictions most often affect "bully-breed" dogs such as the Staffordshire Bull Terrier. Always check to make sure your dog will be welcome wherever you plan to travel, whether it's a city, hotel, or boarding facility.

*Photo Courtesy of
Helena Lehtis*

may be needed while you are away, as well as some flea and worm treatment, to ensure this cover does not lapse during this time. If he is due a vaccine soon, this can also be given to ensure his immunity is up to date, more of which is talked about in Chapter 12.

Before you leave the vet's, check that you have all their contact details on your cell phone, as if your Staffie has an emergency while you are traveling, the attending vet will probably wish to contact your local vet to get his full clinical history. It is also useful to do some research about the vets in the area you are traveling to, and have their contact details saved. That way, you won't waste time trying to find the contact details of a nearby vet in the case of an emergency.

Before you set off on your travels, take some time to check that you have all the accessories that you will need close to hand. Your dog should be wearing a collar with an identity tag on it, detailing your current cell number and address. Some people choose to put their dog's name on the tag too, however this is not necessary, and may cause issues if your Staffie is stolen, as the thief will know the name of your dog to get him to respond to him.

Photo Courtesy of Emma Ceely

Traveling in a Car

Getting used to the car can be a lengthy process for some dogs, whereas others will take to it on their first journey. It is best, however, that your Staffie's first journey in the car is not a long one. Start by allowing him to get used to being in the car on his own terms. Maybe allow him to get in and have a treat or a toy in there, so he begins to associate it with being a nice place.

Taking a short first journey with your Staffie will enable you to see if he is anxious or gets nauseous. Some dogs struggle with travel sickness in the car, which leads to a negative experience for them. They may drool or actually vomit, but the good news is that your veterinarian can provide you with anti-sickness tablets which can be given before a journey, to ensure it goes as smoothly as possible.

Once your Staffie is happy with the car, you can set off on a longer journey. The first thing you must consider is where in the car you will put him. There are several options. In the hatch is a popular option, as then your Staffie does not take up space where humans might need to sit. If you place him in the hatch, it is best to purchase a dog guard which will fit behind the seats to stop him from jumping forward in the car.

Another option, especially if your dog is destructive, is to use a crate, either in the hatch or secured firmly on the seats. You will need a fairly large crate for your Staffie, as it must be large enough for him to stand up, stretch, and lie down without touching the sides. It must have suitable ventilation to allow sufficient airflow through it, so that your dog doesn't get hot, and it is best if it is made of strong material or metal, so that your dog cannot easily escape it.

You don't have to just use the crate in the car either. As noted earlier, you may find it useful in the house to crate your Staffie when you leave or at night, to stop him from chewing on things or causing trouble in the house. If crate trained from the age of a puppy, your Staffie will not see it as a punishment, but rather he will find that the crate is his sanctuary and area of comfort.

Finally, the last option for traveling your dog is to place him on a back seat. This arrangement is only suited to dogs that are not destructive or highly active. It is a safe method of traveling him if you put him in a harness with a seatbelt attachment. That way he will not only be safe in a crash, but he also cannot jump over the seats to join you in the front, potentially causing an accident. However, if you decide this is the way you would like your

Photo Courtesy of
Charlene Plevyak

dog to travel, you may wish to either cover your seats or purchase a dog bed to put on the back seat, as the seats will easily become dirty for future passengers in your car.

When you are traveling a long distance, ensure that all the accessories you need are at hand. Having dog food, water, and a leash easily accessible will make your journey easier. It is recommended that you stop to give your dog food every 12 hours, and water every 4 hours, when traveling. If you are traveling in hot weather and your car is not air conditioned, more frequent stops may be required. Your dog will also appreciate stops every few hours to stretch his legs and toilet if needed.

Traveling by Plane

If you are traveling abroad and wish to take your Staffordshire Bull Terrier with you, it is important that you first check if the airline will accept him. Some airlines have placed the Staffordshire Bull Terrier on the list of restricted breeds, so it is best to contact the airline before you book your tickets, just to make sure.

If the Staffie is not on the list of restricted breeds, and your dog is over 12 weeks, then you are good to go. Each airline has different requirements for traveling with dogs, and so make sure you do your research first. Some airlines allow small dogs to travel in the cabin; however, a small Staffie will probably be borderline size-wise, and so it is best to assume that he will travel in the hold.

When in the hold, your Staffie will need to travel in an airline-approved crate. The guidelines for a crate will be readily available from any airline which accepts dogs. The crate will go in a pressurized, temperature-controlled part of the plane.

When you present your dog at the airport, most airlines will require you to also provide a health certificate from your veterinarian, export paperwork, vaccine records, and passport. It is your responsibility to get all of this in order, and not the airline's or travel agent's.

If it is below 45 degrees Fahrenheit or above 85 degrees Fahrenheit during departure, arrival, and during connections, your dog may be refused travel unless your vet has provided a letter detailing that your dog is used to these conditions. Therefore, traveling at a time of year when the weather is favorable is a good idea.

Vacation Lodging

Photo Courtesy of Tammy Duffy

Once you reach your vacation destination, it is prudent to remember that not everyone at the accommodation may like dogs. Always keep in mind that you should leave the accommodation as you found it, and try to keep your Staffie from causing any disruption to other people's vacations.

If your dog likes to bark, or chews on furniture, it is best not to leave him alone in the accommodation. Separation anxiety can be heightened in unfamiliar circumstances. However, if you have crate trained your Staffie, this is an excellent opportunity to offer it to him. A crate will provide an area that he is familiar with, and will help him feel safe and at home.

When taking your Staffie out and about, always make sure to clean up after him. Some areas of a vacation resort may not allow dogs, even if you are allowed to keep him in the accommodation, and therefore it is worth asking the receptionist when you arrive where you can take him to walk and toilet.

Leaving Your Dog at Home

For some dogs, traveling can be extremely stressful, and it is in both their interest and yours to leave them at home. If you choose this option, there are several different places where you can ensure that your dog gets appropriate care while you are away.

The first option, and the one which many people will choose, is to book him into a boarding kennel. There are many different standards of boarding kennels, from basic kennels, to 5-star luxury dog hotels, to breed-specific kennels, and therefore visiting a few before you book will ensure you choose one which meets your dog's needs. When your dog is boarding at a kennel, he will probably have an enclosure which is part indoors and part outdoors. This enables him to have a space to run and toilet, and another space to eat and sleep. A couple of times a day, the staff will exercise him. This may be by letting him out in a communal play area with other dogs and supervising him, or it may be taking him for a long walk. If you have a rescue

Photo Courtesy of
Jackie Morgan

Staffie, it is likely that your dog will feel strongly one way or another toward kennels; he may be terrified of staying in kennels as it reminds him of the days he was abandoned, or it may be that he is so used to being in kennels that he is very relaxed to be housed in this manner.

If you are hoping for a more one-to-one care plan for your dog while you are away, but are on a budget, the next option would be to have a friend, family member, or the original breeder of your Staffie dog-sit for you. This may be in your home or their home. The benefit of this option is that you know the carer and so does your dog. If the carer has their own dog, this may provide an excellent opportunity for your dog to play and burn off steam while you are away, but ensure that the dogs know each other before dropping your Staffie off, as the other dog may be less enthusiastic about having another dog in their territory.

The final option, which is the most expensive, is to hire a dedicated house- and dog-sitter. These are usually professionals who come and live in your home while you are away. This is an excellent option for your dog, as their environment and routine stay the same. Not only that, it provides security for your house, and you can rest assured that all will be taken care of. The only unknown factor for your dog is the dog-sitter, and therefore it is important to do a meet and greet, ideally on neutral ground, such as a walk in the park.

Whether you choose to take your dog on your travels or leave him behind, there are lots of things to consider when making preparations, but by doing this, you can ensure that you enjoy your travels and vacation to the full.

CHAPTER 9
Nutrition

"Bully breeds in general can have a compromised immune system. I like to boost their immune system with supplements and probiotics and a really good diet. Staffords can really eat anything if this is kept in mind."

Teri Keetch
Dyna Staffs

Importance of Nutrition

It can be very overwhelming to get to the pet store and see so many brands on the shelves. Trying to figure out which food to feed your Staffie can be quite a challenge. After all, food influences a great number of aspects of your dog's health. Food can improve coat, skin, dental, and joint health, but it can also lead to bladder issues, poor growth, or exacerbating underlying conditions.

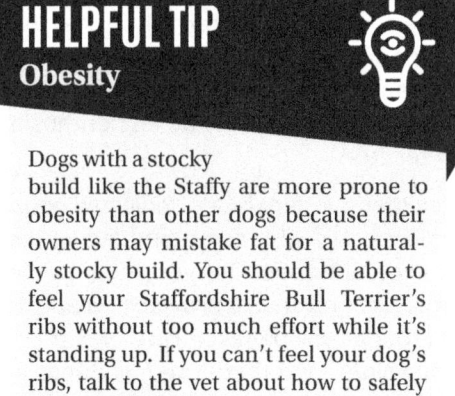

HELPFUL TIP
Obesity

Dogs with a stocky build like the Staffy are more prone to obesity than other dogs because their owners may mistake fat for a naturally stocky build. You should be able to feel your Staffordshire Bull Terrier's ribs without too much effort while it's standing up. If you can't feel your dog's ribs, talk to the vet about how to safely reduce its weight.

It's not as easy as just looking at the packaging to decide which is the best food for your Staffie. What might be good for your dog might not work well for another dog. Therefore, simply going on recommendation alone is not reliable. Nevertheless, other owners, breeders, and even veterinarians commonly feel strongly one way or the other about certain brands of food, and while their knowledge may be valuable, you should look at the whole picture when choosing a food for your Staffie.

Commercial Food

Commercial food is what you will find in pet stores, vet's offices, and supermarkets. There is a wide variety of quality, from foods which will do more harm than good, all the way to extremely good quality, and enriched foods. Remember though, just because a food suits one dog, it does not mean it will suit another, so there are many things you should consider when choosing a food off the shelf for your Staffie.

Dry or Wet

Generally, commercial food can be bought as dry food in packages, or wet food in cans, pouches, or trays. There is no right or wrong choice when it comes to feeding your dog wet or dry food, and many people will feed their dogs a mixture. However, there are pros and cons to both.

Dry foods are more condensed than wet foods, so you will not have to feed as many grams of dry food as you would wet food to ensure your Staffie gets all the nutrients he needs. Because dry food is more condensed than wet food, it can swell when it hits the stomach acid. Before you give it to your dog, you should test how much it swells by adding a cup of water to a cup of dry food and leaving it for half an hour. The less it swells, the better it is for your dog, as swelling can lead to a sense of feeling full and bloated.

Dry food kibble can come in a variety of sizes. The general rule is that you should buy the biggest kibble that your dog will happily take. This is because if the kibble sizes are large, your dog must crunch through them before swallowing. As a result, the teeth have a regular source of abrasion, which reduces the amount of tartar build-up and leads to healthier teeth. This is discussed further in Chapter 10.

Wet food, on the other hand, does not provide abrasion on the teeth, so your Staffie is much more likely to develop dental disease in his lifetime. Nevertheless, there is a place for wet food in a dog's diet. Wet food is usually more palatable than dry food, so if your Staffie is a picky eater, then he is likely to eat more wet food than dry food. Wet food is also much easier to eat, so puppies, or elderly dogs with arthritis in their jaws, will be more easily able to consume wet food.

Puppy Food

If you have bought or rescued a Staffie who is not yet fully grown, he should be fed on a puppy or junior food. These varieties of food are essential to provide the correct nutrients for ongoing growth, bone development, and energy levels. They are higher in protein, calcium, and phosphorus than adult foods. Most mainstream commercial diets will produce puppy or junior variants of their food.

AAFCO Standards

By purchasing a commercial diet, you can ensure that you are purchasing food for your Staffie which has met stringent standards. This ensures that all food which meets the standards is appropriately balanced for the life-stage they are marketing to, and will not be detrimental to dogs who consume it. The Association of American Feed Control Officials (AAFCO) has set out these standards and all commercial pet foods in the US must meet them before they can be sold to the public.

Photo Courtesy of
Michelle Daniels

BARF and Homemade Diets

There has been a recent change in attitude in the general public toward the way that our dogs are being fed. People are more health conscious, and care about the environment. They want to ensure there are no genetically modified organisms or preservatives in their dog's food. And they frequently want the food to be locally sourced, natural, and organic. It is difficult to meet all these criteria with commercial dog food, so it's no surprise that more people are now turning toward cooking food for their dogs at home.

Unfortunately, homemade diets, whether it be a cooked diet or bones and raw food (BARF), are not as healthy as they initially appear to be. Many people claim that their dogs have improved health of the coat, skin, teeth, and general energy, but it certainly doesn't come without risks.

There have now been numerous studies on raw food demonstrating the high numbers of dangerous pathogens which can be transmitted to the dog, and the owner, from these diets. These pathogens include bacteria such as Salmonella, E.coli, and Campylobacter. Not only do they stay in the saliva of the dog, but they are also still present in the feces and transfer to the coat when the dog grooms himself. This means they can be readily transmitted to people. At particular risk are those people who are more vulnerable, such as children and the elderly. In these age groups, infections with these pathogens can be life-threatening. Dogs can also contract these infections, but in general their digestive system is more robust than that of humans.

There are other risks which come with BARF diets which contain whole bones. Bones can present risks of choking, damage to teeth, internal punctures, and internal obstructions. Most raw food advocates will argue that only raw bones are being offered, which are more flexible and digest better than cooked bones, but regardless, there is still some element of risk.

The main concern by veterinarians for BARF and homemade diets is the lack of balancing the diets appropriately. In a study of 95 raw food diets, 60% were found to have a major nutritional balance. The majority of homemade diet feeders will not have consulted an expert veterinary nutritionist, but rather will have developed their dog's diet through personal research or advice from breeders or friends who also feed their dogs homemade diets. As a result, the diet is not balanced properly, and there are excessive levels of calcium and phosphorus or incorrect levels of other nutrients. This can lead to serious consequences in the dogs receiving the diets, and they can develop conditions such as rickets, bladder stones, and stunted growth, particularly if they are not yet fully grown.

Photo Courtesy of
Melissa Rooney and Kevin Sharpe

However, if you are still keen to feed your Staffie a diet which is alternative to the normal commercial foods, there are now several pet food manufacturers who are making homecooked or raw frozen meats, which can be purchased. These meals, which have been prepared by a manufacturer, especially if they contain raw foods, will usually have been balanced with additional minerals and vitamins, as well as tested for toxins and microbes.

Pet Food Labels

So, once you've decided that you want to feed a commercial diet, whether it be wet or dry, you should look at the label on the packaging. A lot can be deciphered from the label if you know where to look. All pet food labels must contain an ingredients list, which is usually in order of weight, and a guaranteed analysis, which details the protein, fiber, moisture, and fat content of the food.

Guaranteed Analysis

The guaranteed analysis, which details the amount of protein, fiber, moisture, and fat content of the food, cannot be compared between wet and dry food directly. Therefore, you will first have to do some calculations to understand the actual levels of these nutrients in the food. This will then provide you with some figures which will allow you to directly compare different foods.

The percentages of the nutrient of interest must be divided by the percentage of food which is dry so that they can be compared. For example:

A wet food with a moisture content of 75% will therefore be 25% dry. If the protein content is 5%, the calculation will be 5/0.25 = 20% protein on a dry matter basis.

A dry food with a moisture content of 10% will therefore be 90% dry. If the protein content is 20%, the calculation will be 20/0.9 = 22.2% protein on a dry matter basis.

Once the dry matter basis has been calculated, the guaranteed analysis is an excellent source of information. In general, a higher protein is a good sign, as it suggests that the food is not bulked up with carbohydrates. Ash and fiber are usually around 3-4% and fat should not be over 15% once the food has been adjusted to take into consideration the moisture content.

Photo Courtesy of
Daz Priestley

Ingredients

There can be many different ingredients which make up dog food, and as long as your Staffie has no allergies, it doesn't matter whether you choose to feed him chicken, beef, salmon, etc.

The list of ingredients will be in order of weight. A dog food should always have a meat protein source as their first ingredient. This way, you know you will not be feeding your Staffie carbohydrate fillers, which he would not naturally be eating in the wild.

When looking at the protein ingredients, there may be three different types: meat, meat by-products (such as offal and chicken legs), or "meals." "Meals," which are dehydrated ground meat, contain almost 300% more protein per gram compared to the fresh meat that they are derived from, and since they are light in weight, they will be further down the ingredients list than if the manufacturer had used the unprocessed meat.

There can be a wide variety of meats used in dog food, such as beef, chicken, turkey, venison, salmon, lamb, or tuna, just to name a few. However, just because a food is labeled as a certain flavor, it does not mean that it contains solely that meat. A chicken flavor dog food can have a small amount of beef in it and still be called chicken.

If your Staffie has allergies, there is a chance that food can be the reason. The ingredients in the food which usually trigger allergies are meat proteins. The common allergens are common meats, such as chicken or beef, and therefore changing to a more novel protein source, such as venison, duck, turkey or tuna, will often alleviate some of the symptoms.

Fish proteins in particular are excellent sources of omega-3 and omega-6 fatty acids. These are useful for ensuring the health of the coat, skin, brain, and joints. In the ratio of 1:3 of omega-3 to omega-6, they can also have anti-inflammatory effects which will help reduce the discomfort associated with allergic inflamed skin and arthritic joints.

Alongside meat ingredients, there are usually carbohydrate and vegetable ingredients too. Carbohydrate ingredients are frequently grain-based, such as barley, oatmeal, brown rice, white rice, or maize. Whole grains in particular are high-quality complex ingredients, which provide fiber, vitamin B, energy, and plenty of minerals. Most dogs have no problem with grains; however, anecdotally it has been recognized that they exacerbate allergies and cause itchy skin. So, if you are unfortunate enough to have a Staffie who suffers from skin allergies, which are discussed further in Chapter 13, then you may wish to consider feeding a grain-free diet.

If the diet is grain free, starchy vegetables are commonly used as the ingredients to make up the carbohydrates. These include potatoes, sweet potatoes, and pumpkin. These keep the immune system healthy with plenty of vitamins B and C, and pumpkin in particular is very good for the digestive system as it is packed full of fiber.

Other common ingredients include carrots and peas. Carrots are high in vitamin A, which is good for healthy skin, coat, eyes, and nerve and muscle function, and they add carbohydrates without adding more grain. Peas are high in fiber, which aids digestion, keeps the guts comfortable, and helps maintain a normal consistency of the stools through control of water balance. They are also high in protein for a vegetable, at over 25%, which has to be kept in mind when working out how much of the protein content comes from meat sources.

Weight Monitoring

Monitoring your Staffie's weight is extremely important, as it can have a major effect on the health of your dog. It is a common sight to see an overweight Staffie, and it is easy to get to that point without intention. Feeding your dog is seen as an act of love for many owners, so the odd tidbit here and there, while meaning well, can cause gradual weight gain over the years if the main meal of the day is not adjusted for it.

Being overweight can have a major toll on the liver in particular. The liver is the organ which produces bile, an important substance to help digest fats. Without effective production of bile, it is easy for dogs to lose weight rapidly. In addition, the liver filters out toxins from the blood, and is involved in bilirubin excretion, a by-product of old red blood cells, so it goes without saying, if the liver is not functioning properly, your Staffie will feel very ill.

Being overweight and chronically overfed can also lead to other diseases, such as diabetes. The pancreas is an organ which produces a hormone called insulin. This helps to reduce the blood sugar levels by uptaking it into cells to be used for energy. Without insulin, the blood sugars reach a dangerously high level, which can result in your Staffie feeling extremely sick.

Another reason to keep your Staffie in tip-top condition is to reduce the stress on his joints. In Chapter 13, we look at how Staffordshire Bull Terriers are prone to joint conditions such as hip and elbow dysplasia, and in Chapter 14, you will read about how arthritis can develop later in life. To give your Staffie the best chance at keeping his joints healthy and pain-free, keeping him slim will definitely help.

So, we know why it is best to keep your Staffie slim, but what is an ideal weight for him? Because of a variety of sizes within the breed, there is no ideal weight that a Staffie should be. It is better to monitor his weight through regularly assessing his body condition score. This is a condition scoring system from one to nine, one being emaciated, and nine being obese. An ideal score is between four and five. The scoring is as follows:

BCS 1 = Extremely underweight. Ribs, lumbar vertebrae, pelvic bones and bony prominences are visible from a distance. Major loss of muscles and no obvious body fat.

BCS 3 = Underweight. Ribs easily felt and may just be visible. Not much fat present. Obvious waist and obviously tucked up abdomen. Some visible bony prominences. Tops of lumbar vertebrae easily seen.

BCS 5 = Ideal weight. Ribs easily felt with minimal fat covering. Waist can be seen when standing behind the dog. Ribs just visible when looking from above the dog. Abdomen tucked up when viewed from the side.

BCS 7 = Overweight. Heavy fat cover over ribs and difficult to feel. Noticeable fat deposits in lumbar region of back and base of tail. Difficulty viewing waist. Slight abdominal tuck.

BCS 9 = Obese. Very large fat deposits over base of tail, spine, and chest. No waist or abdominal tuck. Distended abdomen. Fat deposits around neck and limbs.

Even though the Staffie has a short coat, and so much of these areas are visible, it is still important to feel the areas to fully understand the level of fat covering the bones. With being careful about what you feed your Staffie, along with regularly monitoring your Staffie's weight, you are far more likely to have a healthy dog whose companionship you will be able to enjoy late into his senior years.

CHAPTER 10
Dental Care

What attracts many people to Staffordshire Bull Terriers is their enormous smile, often spanning from ear to ear. Frequently with that comes plenty of excitable panting and licks to your face. However, the last thing you want with all that is a mouth full of rotten teeth and bad breath close to your face. This is just one reason why keeping your dog's oral hygiene in good shape is important.

Importance of Dental Care

It is all too common for owners to neglect the dental hygiene of their dogs' mouths. This often isn't due to purposeful neglect, but rather a misunderstanding about what is required to maintain a healthy mouth. After all, wild dogs never have their mouths inspected or teeth brushed, and they manage to clean their teeth relatively effectively through crunching on bones. This is a common argument used for people keen on feeding their dogs a raw food diet, which was talked about in the previous chapter.

HELPFUL TIP
The Importance of Dental Care

Did you know that your dog's dental health affects its overall health? It sounds crazy, but neglecting your Staffordshire Bull Terrier's dental health could cause heart problems down the road! Giving your Staffy plenty of appropriate things to chew on will help, but it's best if you can brush its teeth daily with toothpaste designed for dogs. Dogs also need regular dental cleanings from the vet to help remove plaque and tartar below the gumline.

However, unfortunately, most of our domestic dogs are no longer eating food which enables their teeth to stay in good condition, and dental disease is extremely common. Some breeds are more prone to it that others, and luckily, Staffies are not one of those breeds. Nevertheless, with a dental care routine, you can prevent your Staffie from having bad breath and rotten teeth, which can lead to oral pain and missing teeth. This routine must be reinforced from a young age though, as otherwise teeth brushing will not be tolerated well.

Dental Anatomy

There are several different parts of the tooth; some of which you can see, and some of which is buried in the gum. The main part of the tooth above the gum is called the crown, and below the gum is called the root. Depending on the type of tooth, it may have one, two or even three roots. Where the crown meets the root is usually around the gum line. This is a particular area of interest, as this is commonly where tartar can build up from poor dental hygiene.

Photo Courtesy of Beth Williams

When a puppy is born, he will have very few teeth. In the weeks to follow, razor-sharp deciduous (baby) teeth begin to erupt. A puppy will eventually have 28 deciduous teeth. Over the first year of life, these fall out and 42 adult teeth come through in their place. Sometimes the deciduous teeth are not pushed out properly by the erupting adult teeth, and need to be removed by a veterinarian.

There are different types of teeth in the various parts of the mouth, all of which have different functions. The incisors are at the very front. These are used for nibbling off flesh close to the bone. Next are the large canines, which would be used during hunting to grab hold of their prey. Finally, along the cheeks are pre-molars and molars. These two types of teeth are flatter and are used for grinding and crushing through harder food.

A tooth is made up of several elements, of which a large part is dentine; a type of bone. Covering the dentine is a layer of enamel, which protects the tooth from the outside environment. In the center of the tooth is a fleshy middle, known as the pulp. This contains many nerves and can be extremely painful if it becomes damaged. The root of the tooth sits in a socket in the jaw bone or skull, and it is held in place by an extremely strong ligament, known as the periodontal ligament.

Tartar Build-up and Gingivitis

Tartar, which is also commonly referred to as plaque, is when food material and bacteria build up around the area where the crown, root, and gums all meet. This happens more commonly when a dog is fed on a wet food diet alone. The gums contain many blood vessels, and therefore inflammatory cells flock to the area. This is in reaction to the bacteria which is in contact with the gums, but it can cause significant pain. The inflammation of the gums is known as gingivitis. Gingivitis can further progress to periodontal disease, whereby the periodontal ligament becomes weak from the inflammation, and no longer holds the teeth in place, resulting in tooth loss.

Tooth loss does not happen overnight, and therefore the tooth is usually wobbly for an extended period of time before it finally falls out. This means whenever your dog chews on something hard, it causes significant discomfort in that area. For some dogs, this causes them to lose weight as they do not want to eat as much, whereas for other dogs, they will happily continue to eat, despite the discomfort and foul taste in their mouth. Staffies usually love their food and fall into the second of those categories.

To prevent gingivitis, you must first prevent the tartar build-up. Treatment of tartar build up can be done, but often it requires a dental procedure, more of which is talked about later in the chapter.

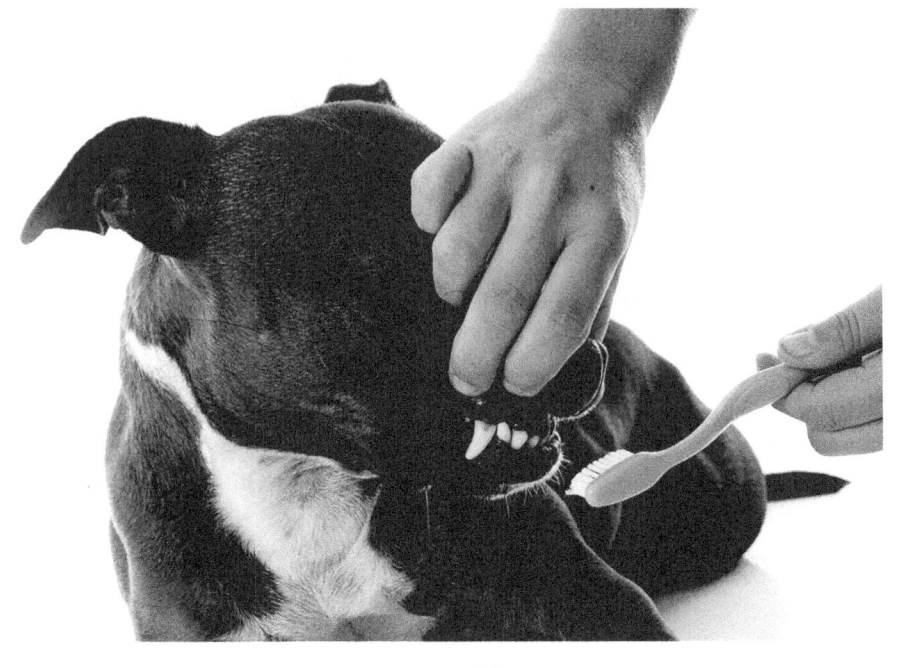

Dental Care

Caring for your Staffie's teeth is best approached from several different angles. There is not one best method of keeping your dog's teeth clean, but rather it is best to use multiple methods to maintain sparkly white teeth and fresh breath. Dental care should become part of a daily routine, started from the puppy stage, as this will prevent deterioration of the mouth. However, if you have only acquired your Staffie at an older age, maybe through a rescue center, it is never too late to start ensuring he has clean teeth, as even though you may not return his mouth to that of a puppy's, it will definitely prevent any further build-up of tartar and reduce gingivitis.

Teeth Brushing

All owners should brush their dog's teeth every day. This is a tall order for many people, but putting in some effort will benefit your Staffie greatly over the course of his lifetime. Brushing teeth will help to keep them clean, reduce the amount of tartar, and keep the breath fresh. It will also ensure that you are checking the mouth on a regular basis and any changes can be picked up early.

To brush your dog's mouth, you will need a toothbrush and toothpaste. This can be added to your list of things to buy in Chapter 3. You cannot use regular toothpaste, however, as this can be highly toxic to dogs leading to erratic blood glucose levels and liver damage. Anyway, your dog will much prefer the meaty taste of a dog toothpaste, which you can buy off the internet, at veterinary practices, and many pet stores. Dog toothpaste works through enzymatic action. This is when enzymes in the toothpaste work to dissolve any new tartar build up on the surface of the teeth, thereby reducing bacteria and freshening breath.

Ideally, the best method of applying toothpaste is with a toothbrush. You can buy dog toothbrushes which are shaped for easy use, and firmer than human toothbrushes. However, finger toothbrushes also work well if a dog toothbrush is not tolerated. For dogs which are older and not used to having their teeth brushed, smearing the toothpaste on the teeth is better than not using the toothpaste at all as the enzymatic action alone will help to dissolve tartar. Ensure that all the teeth are covered, including the small incisors at the front and the molars right at the back. The muscular cheeks of your Staffie will need to be pulled right back to reach these teeth.

When you are done with brushing your dog's teeth, ensure it is followed with plenty of positive reinforcement. More sensitive dogs, or dogs which are not used to it, can find brushing teeth a little stressful, so the more positive you are, the more your Staffie will come to accept it.

Dental Chews

Dental chews are a nice way of keeping your dog's teeth healthy, and a way which he is sure to appreciate. Your dog won't be aware that this delicious treat is actually for his benefit. It is important to note that although giving dental chews is much easier than brushing, they are not a replacement for brushing. They should always be used in combination.

Dental chews are formed to provide some form of abrasion or friction to the surface of the tooth so that tartar is broken or sucked off. As with all treats, they are not calorie free, and so calculating how many calories must be taken out of your dog's normal food is important to do. Otherwise, you may end up with a rather overweight Staffie.

Some owners will find regular dental chews too unhealthy and would rather opt for a more natural type of chew. These options typically include bones, antlers, and pig ears. Be aware that since these are all hard, if swallowed they can lead to life-threatening blockages of the intestine. Therefore, if given, you should supervise your Staffie at all times. Out of these options, antlers are the safest to give your dog. Not only does your dog not ingest anything, and therefore you don't need to worry about extra calories, antlers do not splinter like bones and therefore the risk of gastric blockages or perforations are significantly reduced. Also, antlers do not smell and last much longer than other natural treats.

Dental Wash

Dental wash is easy to add to your dog's daily routine. Much like human mouthwash, it must be used daily to make a difference. When using dog mouthwash, you do not need to rinse the mouth with it every day. Instead, it can be added to the drinking water, as long as the drinking water is changed daily. You should never consider using human mouthwash, as like human toothpaste, it is toxic to dogs and can cause internal organ damage.

Dental wash works in a similar manner to toothpaste. It contains enzymes which help dissolve the newly built-up tartar on the teeth. It won't, however, break down the tartar which has been accumulating for a while. Dental wash can come in a variety of flavors, but mint is a popular one. Some dogs do not like this flavor in their drinking water, so you should monitor for water intake to ensure he is still getting plenty of fluids.

Dental Food

There are several dental dog foods available on the market from leading manufacturers which are proving to be highly effective. Dental food only comes in a dry kibble form, as wet food has no positive effect on the teeth. The way it works is the kibble sizes are quite large, which requires the dog to bite through them with some effort before being able to swallow the food. The kibble pieces have a texture which creates abrasion against the edge of the tooth, thereby removing some tartar build-up.

If your dog has great teeth, there is no need to change his diet to a dental diet. Instead, a normal dry food is usually sufficient to manage tartar build-up.

Dental Procedures

Hopefully with the above dental care from a young age, you will never have to have a dental procedure done on your dog. However, if you have only taken on an older dog, or you have not been consistent with your dog's dental care, he may need a dental procedure at some point. Every year, when you take your dog to the vet for his annual vaccine booster, your vet should check the teeth. He will be able to recommend whether a dental procedure will be beneficial.

Dental procedures are rarely difficult, and any general practice vet will be able to perform them in their veterinary practice. Most vet practices will perform dental procedures on a daily basis, and so most vets will have plenty of experience in this.

A dental procedure is a day procedure and your Staffie will not be away from you for more than the day, as long as there are no complications. The procedure will require a general anesthetic, as dental tools can be sharp and trying to use them on a wiggly, excitable, conscious Staffie is a disaster waiting to happen.

You will need to drop off your dog in the morning, having not had any breakfast as the anesthetic can cause dogs to feel nauseous. Once your dog has been given the anesthetic, the vet will start by scaling the teeth. This removes all the tartar and will enable the vet to fully assess the junction where the crown meets the root. Next, he will run a probe around the roots of the teeth, and if there are any pockets in the periodontal ligament or wobbly teeth, these then must be removed.

Photo Courtesy of
Shelby Hanby

To remove a tooth, first the periodontal ligament needs to be weakened and broken. This is done by using a tool called an elevator. Once the tooth is loose, gentle traction will be used to pull the tooth out. Sometimes the vet will close the socket with a stitch, and sometimes it will be kept open, depending on the health of the mouth, in terms of bacterial burden, and how big the hole is.

After your Staffie's dental procedure, if he has had teeth out, he may need soft food for a few days; however, his mouth will be significantly more comfortable than it was previously, regardless of what is being fed. Your vet may want to recheck the mouth a few days later to make sure the sockets are healing well.

Prevention is always better than cure, so even though your vet can make your Staffie's mouth look like a puppy's again, keeping your Staffie's mouth in good condition from puppyhood is always a better option. With diligent dental care from the outset, you can ensure your Staffie has a healthy, painless mouth with fresh breath.

CHAPTER 11
Grooming

About the Coat

Staffordshire Bull Terriers are excellent dogs for those wishing to do minimal grooming. Their coat is short and low maintenance, and regardless of how much or little you brush it, it will always look and lie the same. The coat is flat to the skin, and usually fairly coarse. It can come in six color varieties: solid red, fawn, white, black, blue, or brindle, or sometimes a mix of several of these colors.

Despite the coat being short, it still sheds year-round, even during winter. Therefore, while your house will have significantly less hair on the floor compared to a long-coated breed, it will still require vacuuming regularly. It also means that your Staffie may not be suitable for people that are allergic to dogs, although allergies to dogs are often related to the dander in the coat, rather than the coat itself.

Coat Health

Keeping the coat in good order is not a challenge when it comes to Staffies. A brush-through once every few days with a bristle brush to remove the dead hair will be sufficient to minimize shedding.

The coat of a Staffie should not naturally smell, so bathing should only be done as needed. Bathing too regularly can strip the coat of natural oils and dry out the skin, leaving it to be less waterproof and impervious to challenges of the environment. A quick rinse down after a muddy walk, and a full shampoo bath once every couple of months, is all that is required.

With that being said, Staffies are prone to skin allergies, which is discussed further in Chapter 13. If you have a dog with skin allergies, normal dog shampoo should not be used, as it can worsen the symptoms. Instead, shampoo recommended by your vet should be used, and this usually has anti-bacterial properties too. The reason why this is particularly important for a dog with allergies is because the skin barrier is not as effective as a normal dog's skin against the regular commensal bacteria on the skin; thus, skin infections are significantly more common in dogs suffering from allergies.

*Photo Courtesy of
Bethany Hughes*

External Parasites

There are several different types of external parasites that can make their homes in your Staffie's coat. Once they have done so, it can be a challenge to get rid of them. Therefore, prevention is always better than cure.

The market is flooded with anti-parasitic treatments and preventions, so it is sometimes overwhelming to know which ones to get. It is best to allow your vet to take the lead and advise you on the most suitable products for your dog. Products bought from the pet store are also usually less effective than those bought from the vet, as vets will be able to sell ones which are more potent and have less resistance to them.

There are several different parasites which you may want to consider providing cover for. Fleas are the ones which usually come first to people's minds. Fleas are parasites which hop around and feed on the blood of your Staffie. Their bites can be extremely itchy. What most people are not aware of, though, is 95% of fleas live in the environment rather than on the dog, so if your dog has a problem, your house does also. Therefore, if you are treating for fleas that you have already seen on your dog, as well as giving a product to your dog to prevent fleas, you should also treat your house. You can do this by washing all bedding in hot water, vacuuming thoroughly, especially in areas which are dark and warm, and spraying the house with flea insecticide spray. This will have to be done monthly for three months to get on top of an outbreak, as the products do not kill unhatched eggs, so repetitive treatments will kill off the larvae after they have hatched before they mature into adults.

Ticks are also external parasites which you may wish to apply products for, to either prevent or treat. Ticks are commonly found in areas of woodland or long grasses, especially where wildlife such as deer are also found. If you live in an area like this, having a long-lasting tick prevention collar on your dog will ensure that the protective cover does not lapse if you forget to apply a treatment. If your dog gets a tick, you may only notice it after it has been there a couple of days, and significantly swelled from sucking blood. Ticks can transmit diseases such as Lyme disease, tick paralysis, and babesia, but these are uncommon. It is more likely that a tick will cause a local skin infection in the area of the bite, and therefore should be removed as soon as it is found. This can be easily done with a tick twister fork. Place the fork pieces either side of the head of the tick, under the body, then twist and pull. Do not try to remove the tick with tweezers, as it usually ends up with the head breaking off and being left in. This can lead to infections and abscesses. If you are unsure about removing a tick yourself, your local vet or vet nurse will be happy to help.

Photo Courtesy of
Kieran Tidyman

HELPFUL TIP
Brushing

The best brush to use on your Staffy is a rubber curry-style brush. Going over your dog with one of these brushes once a week will help remove loose hair and spread your dog's natural oils. This will help your Staffordshire Bull Terrier shed less and look shiny.

Other external parasites you may also wish to protect against or treat are lice or mites. These are far less common than fleas and ticks, and are likely to be picked up if your Staffie has been close to an infected animal, which is usually wildlife. A particular mite of concern is that can be picked up in this way is the Sarcoptes scabiei mite that causes sarcoptic mange, usually transmitted by foxes. Some spot-on preventative treatments for fleas also guard against sarcoptic mange, but these are the prescription-only treatments available from your vet, rather than the cheaper products sold at the supermarket.

Demodectic mange, on the other hand, is not contracted from another animal, but occurs when one of the naturally resident mites on a dog's skin, Demodex canis, grows out of control, usually due to a weakened immune system. This is a condition that should always receive veterinary attention.

External parasite treatments can come in several forms, and the one you choose is down to personal preference and ease of administration in your dog. There are spot-on pipettes, which go on the skin on the back of the neck, tablets, chewy treats, collars, sprays, and shampoos. Each brand will have a different length of efficacy, and therefore do not assume every one needs to be applied monthly.

Nail Clipping

Nail clipping is an essential part of your dog's maintenance. Without regular clipping, the nails can grow excessively long, and either curl around and cut into the pads of the paw, or catch in places and cause toe sprains. It is best to accustom your Staffie to nail clipping from a very young age, as if they are only first introduced to nail clipping later on, you may find it makes them nervous. If you have rescued an adult Staffie, then this is likely to be something you will have to contend with. It is best to take it slowly, and first get him used to the idea of having his feet picked up and fiddled with, before progressing to clipping the nails.

To clip the nails, you will want to buy a nail clipper from your local pet store. These come in a variety of sizes; a large one will be most appropriate for your Staffie, as they tend to have quite large, thick nails.

The nails are made out of keratin, much like our nails. In the center is a fleshy quick, which contains nerves and blood vessels. If the nails are cut too short, then it is easy to catch the quick and cause the nail to bleed. This can be very sore, and a bad experience like this is something your dog may remember for next time. If your dog has clear nails, you can usually see the quick, but if they are black it can be much harder to determine where it is. For some dogs, you can turn the paw upside down, as sometimes the keratin does not completely enclose the quick, and therefore you can see it. For other dogs though, the keratin can completely enclose it, and therefore all you can do is slowly cut small bits off, and be conservative. If you do accidentally catch the quick, do not panic; just apply a firm pressure with a wad of cotton wool for five minutes. If you are not sure about clipping the nails yourself, you can ask your vet, vet nurse, or local groomer to do it for you.

You will not need to clip the nails so frequently if they are kept naturally short. This can be done by walking your dog frequently on harder ground such as concrete and pavements.

Ear Cleaning

Ears are usually self-cleaning, so for many Staffies, you will not have to clean them on a regular basis. However, if your Staffie loves to swim, puts his head down holes, or suffers from skin allergies, he may be more susceptible to having dirty and inflamed ears, which can lead to ear infections. Routine cleaning can help avoid this. Ultimately, you should clean your dog's ears as frequently as your vet recommends it, but a good recommendation is to clean them after every time your dog goes for a swim in a dirty lake, or once every couple of weeks if your Staffie suffers from skin allergies.

Ear cleaner serves several purposes. It removes build up of wax and debris, as well as ensures the environment of the ear is at a pH where bacteria and yeast do not grow. There are many ear cleaners on the market, but your local vet practice will sell a veterinary-approved brand.

To clean the ear, lift up the flap of the ear and insert the nozzle into the ear canal. Give a generous squeeze of the bottle, then place the flap of the ear over the exit of the ear canal so the ear cleaner cannot leak out. Give the ear a massage for about a minute, then let go and stand back. Your dog will most likely shake his head, and this is a good thing, as it brings all the wax to the top of the ear canal. Once this has happened, you can gently wipe it away with some cotton wool, and repeat with the other side.

Photo Courtesy of Holly Arrow

Anal Glands

If you have ever smelled a dog with filled up anal glands, you will never forget it. Anal glands have a distinct, gruesome fishy odor to them, and if they have become full or impacted, your dog will find it very uncomfortable. You may notice him dragging his bottom along the floor to relieve himself of them, or licking his back end constantly. If you are particularly unfortunate, you may find one or more extremely strong-smelling stains on your dog's bedding or your sofa, which will indicate he has an anal gland problem.

The anal glands are two redundant sacs which sit at 4 and 8 o'clock just inside the anus. If your dog has had loose stools recently, or his anal glands are abnormal in shape or position, then fecal material can easily become stuck in them. This leads to impactions and abscesses if not addressed.

Your vet, vet nurse, or groomer can empty your Staffie's anal glands for you by gently inserting a finger into the anus and squeezing them. Most groomers will check the anal glands routinely during a grooming visit, although this is not necessary if your dog rarely has issues with them. However, if you find that your Staffie is frequently having anal gland impactions, keeping them as empty as possible with routine checks, as well as increasing the fiber in his diet with fiber supplements to keep the stools firm, will greatly help his comfort.

Overall, Staffordshire Bull Terriers are easy dogs to maintain when it comes to grooming; however, some work is required at home to keep on top of his general coat, ear, and nail health. The Staffie can be prone to skin allergies, but in all other cases, this is a low-maintenance breed, and trips to the groomer's are more a matter of preference than a necessity.

CHAPTER 12
Preventative Veterinary Medicine

While you may be lucky and have a dog that spends very little time at the vet's, there is always the chance that you find yourself with a Staffie that has a personality which causes him to end up at the vet's fairly frequently. Chewing up toys and swallowing them, eating an entire fruit cake stolen from the counter, and running through bushes or barbed wire and getting injured are all common scenarios. Therefore, it is a good idea to find a vet from the outset that you like and trust. This chapter will help you understand your options when it comes to choosing a vet, and getting preventative treatments.

Choosing a Veterinarian

Choosing a veterinarian is as important as choosing a doctor. You will want to find one that you can trust, who has a nice demeanour around your Staffie, and who is available when you need them. You should always be looking within a short drive of your home, as sometimes you may need to get your dog to the vet in a hurry. Plus, for routine appointments, it is more convenient if your vet is local. But there are many other factors to consider when choosing a veterinarian, from cost, to knowledge, to services and more.

Photo Courtesy of
Ian Dawson

Finances

Veterinary expenses are not cheap, so finding an affordable veterinarian may be high on your priority list. With that being said, you will often get what you pay for, and a more expensive veterinarian may have more experience or better equipment to work with. Prices often differ between chain veterinary practices and independent veterinary practices. Large corporate chain practices, which are run from a headquarters, will have fewer overhead costs as they are dispersed across the whole company. They will also be able to order in bulk and usually have deals with drug companies to keep their prices low. They also may run companywide specials, such as "dental week" or "lump awareness week" where you have free dental or lump checks.

HELPFUL TIP
Pet Insurance

While Staffordshire Bull Terriers are somewhat healthier than other dog breeds, you never know if or when your dog will have an accident or become seriously ill. Pet insurance can help offset major medical costs. However, there are usually waiting periods before the coverage becomes effective, and preexisting conditions are always excluded, so it's crucial to get a pet insurance plan as soon as possible after bringing your Staffy home.

Independent veterinary practices are usually a little more expensive than the chain practices, however in these types of practice, you will find there is a family-run vibe in the building, and usually staff with more experience that have been working in the practice for a large part of their careers.

It is also worth looking into whether your potential new vet practice offers any monthly rates to keep on top of your preventative treatments. Some will arrange a deal where you can pay a monthly premium, and that covers your vaccines, deworming treatments, flea treatments, and a discount off food and services. This is a useful deal to subscribe to, as it saves a lot of money in the long run, and also reminds you to regularly treat your Staffie.

After Hours

You will find quite a variety of approaches to after-hours services in different veterinary practices. Some will provide after-hours services all night, some will provide services into the evening and then switch over to an external provider, and others will use an after-hours service provider all night and weekend.

Photo Courtesy of
Ffion Stapleton

Everybody will have their individual preferences as to what option they prefer. The good thing about having your vet provide after-hours services is that you know who you are going to be dealing with. It will be a familiar environment for your dog and so some of the stress, in a stressful situation in the middle of the night, will be taken away.

Nevertheless, an external provider also has its benefits. While you will have to go to an unfamiliar vet practice and see an unfamiliar face, vets who work for specialist after-hours providers are often specialists in emergency and critical care. They also only work night or weekend shifts, which means they will be fresher than your local vet providing the service. Unfortunately, external providers are frequently more expensive than if a local vet provided the after-hours services.

Specialists

Vet practices can vary greatly in staff numbers, as well as in experience. Some practices will be simple one-man-bands, whereas others may have teams of 15 or more vets working under one roof. With the larger number of staff members, there is also the potential for more variation in experience. Some vets may be newly graduated, whereas others may have specialist qualifications. It is always convenient to visit a practice which employs vets with extra qualifications in fields such as ophthalmology, orthopedics, and cardiology, as if your Staffie ever has a problem, he can be seen to and treated in a familiar vet practice. This saves the need for referral to a specialist center.

Extra Services

Some veterinary practices also offer extra services, which may or may not be of interest to you. These could include grooming services, boarding, nurse consultations, weight clinics, diabetic clinics, and puppy classes. Having access to these services is a great opportunity to bring your dog to the vets for a positive experience, rather than just when he's unwell or needs his annual vaccination.

Vaccinations

All dogs should have vaccinations, as there are some deadly diseases out in the dog world, and therefore it is negligent not to vaccinate your dog. Most puppy classes and boarding kennels will require any dog attending to be up to date with their core vaccinations. Despite this, there are some people who feel strongly against vaccines. If this is you, it is worth allowing your puppy to at least have his initial course of vaccinations, and then do a blood test every year to check that his immunity levels are still sufficient.

The initial vaccine course will vary depending on the brand of the vaccine, but in general, it will require two or three injections, roughly 3-4 weeks apart. After that, an annual booster vaccination is all that is needed to keep up the immunity. The following diseases are routinely vaccinated against:

- Distemper – This vaccination is in the form of an injection. Distemper is a disease which causes coughing, sneezing, vomiting, diarrhoea, lethargy, and reddened eyes, before it spreads to the brain and causes symptoms such as seizures. It also causes hardening of the pads and the nose.

- Hepatitis – This vaccination is in the form of an injection. Hepatitis is an inflammation of the liver caused by Canine Adenovirus. This causes symptoms such as abdominal pain, lethargy, diarrhea, vomiting, enlarged lymph nodes, loss of appetite, swelling of the brain, and eventually death.

- Parvovirus – This vaccination is in the form of an injection. Parvovirus is a life-threatening disease that is common among puppies. It causes profuse bloody diarrhea and occasionally vomiting. Puppies die rapidly of dehydration. It is extremely contagious.

Photo Courtesy of
Margaret Pilawa

Photo Courtesy of Tammy Duffy

- Leptospirosis – This vaccination is in the form of an injection. Up to four strains are vaccinated against depending on the vaccine brand. Dogs come into contact with Leptospirosis through contaminated water. It affects the kidneys, liver, central nervous system, and reproductive system and causes symptoms such as vomiting, diarrhea, lethargy, fever, and yellowing of the skin and eyes.

- Parainfluenza and Bordetella – These vaccinations are given in combination in a vaccine which squirts up a nostril of the dog. Together they form a complex disease called Kennel Cough. This is a highly contagious respiratory disease which causes an inflamed trachea, a hacking cough, and copious phlegm.

- Rabies – This vaccination is in the form of an injection. In rabies endemic areas, it is vital that this vaccination is given. Rabies is a very dangerous virus which can be transmitted to humans through bites. It causes excessive drooling, aggression, and behaviour changes which rapidly progress to death within a week for 100% of cases showing clinical symptoms.

While this seems like a lot of vaccinations, most manufacturers will combine the first four into one injection, so that your dog does not seem like a pin cushion.

Photo Courtesy of
Christine Wilson

Microchipping

Microchipping is a vital part of caring for your dog. Should your dog get lost, stolen or run away, he could easily lose an identity tag on a collar; however, he cannot lose a microchip which has been implanted.

Microchips are small pieces of metal about the size of a small grain of rice, inserted underneath the skin in the region of the shoulder blades. As it is scanned, a unique number is revealed. This number is registered to your details with the microchip company, and therefore you can easily be reunited with your dog.

As discussed in Chapter 8, microchips are only useful if you keep your details up to date with the microchip manufacturers. If you change cell phone number or move house, then it is your responsibility to let the microchip company know.

If you have rescued a dog, there is a strong chance that your Staffie will have been microchipped by the charity or the previous owner. This will not be registered in your name initially, but instead it will be registered in the name of the rescue organization. Most rescue organizations require you to keep the microchip in their name for several months until a trial period has ended, after which you can change the details to your name.

Internal Parasites

Part of your routine care for your Staffie should be to provide him with preventative treatment for internal parasites such as roundworms and tapeworms. This can be done through giving him a tablet, worming treat, or spot-on pipette on the back of the neck.

You may find that some flea treatments also contain treatments for roundworms, so it is important to consult your vet to ensure you do not double dose.

Deworming should be done every three months if your Staffie scavenges or every six months if he doesn't. This is because he is far more likely to pick up a dead animal full of worms if he snuffles up things while out on a walk. The exception to this is if you live in an area where lungworms are prevalent. These can be found inside snails and slugs, which despite seeming grotesque to us, some dogs love to eat! If you do live in one of these areas, deworming with a monthly roundworm treatment will provide your dog with preventative cover for this.

Neutering

Whether or not you decide to neuter your Staffie is a personal preference; however, there are major health benefits to it if you are not wanting to breed from him or her.

Neutering a male dog is called castration. The stereotypical image of a Staffordshire Bull Terrier is him standing with a male owner, wearing a leather, studded collar or harness, and two very prominent testicles on show. However, you do not need to keep to this macho image, and your dog may thank you for it if you don't.

There are many benefits to castrating a male dog, both in terms of general health and behavior. If castrated young, your Staffie will not have yet felt the urge or learned any anti-social behaviors. These can include inter-dog aggression, marking territories, trying to be dominant in the household and constantly on the lookout for females in estrus. Castrating a dog can reduce or prevent all of these behaviors unless you choose to castrate him later on in life, by which time they will be engrained and a behaviorist may need to be consulted to manage them.

In addition to reducing unwanted behaviors, castrating a dog can eliminate many different health risks, such as testicular cancer, prostate cancer, and prostate hyperplasia.

The castration procedure is extremely quick and easy for a vet to do. Most procedures only require a half day visit to the vets, and your dog will be back to normal the next day, unaware of anything that happened to him.

Neutering a female dog is known as spaying. There are even more benefits to spaying a female dog, and therefore all non-breeding females should be spayed. The spay procedure is more invasive than the castration procedure though, as it requires for your Staffie to have an incision into her abdomen. This can be done normally, or laparoscopically, depending on the equipment and experience of your veterinarian. A normal spay procedure will result in a larger incision, and it will remove both the ovaries and the uterus, whereas a laparoscopic spay will only take out the ovaries and will leave a very small incision, but the surgical time is much longer.

The benefits of a spay are numerous, including significantly reducing the risk of mammary cancers, and eliminating the risk of ovarian cancers, uterine cancers, and life-threatening uterus infections known as pyometras. Laparoscopic spays, while they leave the uterus in, will also eliminate the risk of pyometras, as pyometras are driven by hormones which will be absent after the ovaries are taken out. It will also eliminate the risk of unwanted pregnancies and unwanted attention from male dogs. Once your female Staffie has been spayed, she will also no longer have seasons, which can be messy in the home and prevent socialization during her season.

Unfortunately, with spaying comes a risk of side effects, the most common of which is leaking urine later in life. This is called Urethral Sphincter Mechanism Incompetence (USMI). The urethral sphincter is a muscular band closing the exit to your dog's bladder. It has more tone the more estrogen it has come into contact with. This means that female dogs who have been spayed, especially those which were spayed prior to their first season, have more risk of developing USMI later in life. The good news is that it can be successfully controlled with a daily medication, available from your vet.

Pet Insurance

When you first acquire your Staffie, whether from the age of a puppy or as an adult, the first thing you should do is set up pet insurance. Veterinary bills can run into thousands of dollars, and these bills commonly come unexpectedly.

There are several different types of insurance policies, so reading the fine print is important. The first type of policy which is commonly offered is a pot of money per condition. This pot lasts for a lifetime, but once you reach that amount, you will not be able to claim anything else for that condition. Another type of policy also is a sum of money, and that sum of money per condition is renewed every year. Finally, you may find insurance policies that offer a certain amount of money in total every year, rather than per condition. These different types of policies will vary greatly in monthly premiums, so carefully researching which is the best for your budget is a good idea.

Unfortunately, if you rescue an older dog, you may find that your insurance premiums are higher. This is because the insurance company is taking on more risk, as elderly dogs tend to have more conditions wrong with them. You may be able to bring down the cost of the insurance by increasing the excess payment which you are willing to spend, but in the long run, this does not always save you money.

Pet insurance will take away much of the worry of providing for your dog, because if something unexpected arises, you know that he will be covered. Therefore, by purchasing pet insurance, and providing the preventative veterinary measures which have been outlined in this chapter, you can ensure that you are giving your dog every opportunity to live a healthy, happy life.

CHAPTER 13
Diseases and Conditions

As with all pedigree dogs in comparison to cross-breeds, inevitably there will have been some inbreeding of closely linked relatives. Unfortunately, this can lead to poor genetics being accentuated in the DNA and an overrepresentation of certain diseases within the breed. Because of the Staffie's diverse heritage and genetics, generally they are quite a healthy breed; however, there are some conditions which are more common than others. In this chapter, we will explore the different conditions which the Staffordshire Bull Terrier is prone to.

Hip and Elbow Dysplasia

Joint dysplasia of the hip or elbow is a common condition in pedigree breeds of dog, and the Staffie is no different. The hip is a ball and socket joint where the head of the femur (ball) fits into a socket in the pelvis. Normally this should be a perfect match, like pieces of a puzzle, but when a dog has hip dysplasia either the ball or the socket is malformed. When the shapes don't match well, it means the joint is less stable when it moves. In severe cases of hip dysplasia, the ball can luxate out of the hip socket as it moves, resulting in a wobbly, swaying gait if viewed from behind.

Elbow dysplasia, on the other hand, has many different elements to it. It is not as simple a joint as the hip, and within the elbow dysplasia condition, there can be multiple abnormalities in development. The most common issue in elbow dysplasia is osteochondrosis dissecans (OCD). This is when a flap of joint cartilage separates from the surface. In addition to this, several projections can become detached. These are known as an ununited anconeal process (UAP) and a fragmented medial coronoid process (FMCP). This ultimately leads to lameness or an unusual gait.

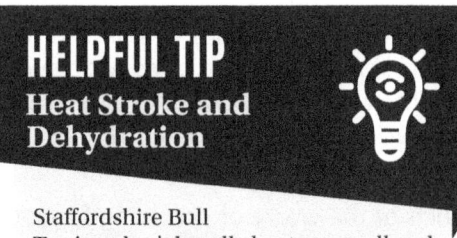

HELPFUL TIP
Heat Stroke and Dehydration

Staffordshire Bull Terriers don't handle heat very well and are prone to overheating, becoming dehydrated, or having heat stroke. Always make sure your Staffy has access to clean water and shade and avoid exercising it during the hottest part of the day.

Photo Courtesy of
Leah Hill

Photo Courtesy of Ian Dawson

Joint dysplasia is usually diagnosed based on X-rays or arthroscopy; however, most veterinarians can have a firm idea that a dog may be suffering from either hip or elbow dysplasia from a simple clinical exam. Joint dysplasia is an inherited condition, and therefore it is usually diagnosed from a young age. X-rays can confirm dysplasia as soon as a dog is fully grown. It is best to understand whether a dog has dysplasia or not from a young age, as if it goes undetected then arthritis will set in at an early stage. This can be mitigated with lifestyle changes, such as keeping your dog controlled on walks with minimal jumping, and physical therapies, such as hydrotherapy, to build up muscle. Joint supplements also aid in maintaining joint health. The weight of the dog also plays a big role in managing the joints, as a lighter dog will have less gravitational force on the joints, and therefore less stress. Inevitably, all dogs that have joint dysplasia will one day get arthritis; the aim is to avoid this for as long as possible.

For severe cases of both elbow and hip dysplasia, surgery is an option to improve the joint. In elbow dysplasia, surgery usually involves removal of bone or cartilage fragments. Sometimes an UAP can be reattached with the use of screws, if surgery is done at a very young age. With hip dysplasia, the hip joint can be modified by removing the head of the femur, reshaping it and replacing it, or taking it out completely. With both hip and elbow dysplasia, total joint replacement is the gold standard surgical treatment, but with implants comes a high cost, as this surgery requires immense skill of the surgeon and expensive implant parts.

Prevention is always better than cure, so buying a puppy from a breeder who has had the parents' joints X-rayed and scored will help you avoid purchasing from poor genetics. Hip and elbow scoring can be done through the British Kennel Club in the UK and PennHIP at the University of Pennsylvania in the US.

Patella Luxation

The Staffordshire Bull Terrier can be prone to another joint condition too, known as patella luxation. The patella is more colloquially known as the knee cap. It is a section of bone, attached by multiple ligaments which runs in a smooth groove at the end of the femur. Normally this groove has high enough sides to it so that the patella stays within the groove, but when a dog is suffering from patella luxation, the inner (known as the medial) side of the groove is too shallow. This causes the patella to slip out of the groove to the inside of the knee joint.

In some cases, the patella will automatically slip back in as the dog moves his joint, whereas others will stay luxated. Due to this, patella luxation is graded on a scale of one to four, with one being extremely mild, and four being when the patella is stuck in a luxated position. Commonly, grade one patella luxation is found incidentally at an examination by a veterinari-

Photo Courtesy of
Kelly Harvey

Photo Courtesy of William J Henrie

an during the annual check-up, as it rarely causes lameness, and therefore goes unnoticed by the owners. The only clinical sign that some dogs may exhibit is an occasional skip in their stride when they run. Grade four, however, is more obvious and causes a mechanical lameness as the dog cannot use his joint appropriately.

Diagnosis comes in two parts; manipulation and X-rays. A veterinarian can easily manipulate the patella to understand how severe the patella luxation is. Once patella luxation is confirmed, an X-ray will be done to understand the level of deterioration of the joint, as arthritis commonly ensues. Depending on how healthy the joint is on X-ray, there will be several options for treatment. Most grade one patella luxation cases are treated conservatively with joint supplements and weight management to minimize unnecessary stress on the joint. Grade two to four are more commonly treated with surgery. There are several techniques that a veterinary surgeon might use, and one is not more beneficial than another. The vet may choose to deepen the patella groove. This technique is called a wedge trochleoplasty. Another technique is known as a lateral transposition of the tibial tubercle, which is when the patella tendon insertion point is moved toward the outside of the leg, creating more pull in the opposite direction. The final technique, and newest developed, is placement of an implant on the inside of the groove to heighten the inside ridge, thereby making it significantly harder for the patella to slip out.

Cataracts

Hereditary cataracts are a common genetic problem in Staffordshire Bull Terriers and approximately 8% of Staffies carry the gene. DNA tests can be done to screen stud dogs for this condition with a blood test or cheek swab, to avoid breeding puppies which may go on to develop cataracts.

Whereas most dogs are susceptible to developing cataracts at an elderly age, hereditary cataracts can begin to develop in the first few months of life, and lead to complete vision loss by two to three years old. A cataract is when the lens in the eye begins to become opaque, and stops light from being able to hit the back of the eye to be processed by the brain.

Luckily, hereditary cataracts are a recessive gene, and therefore both the parents must have the gene and pass it to the offspring for the offspring

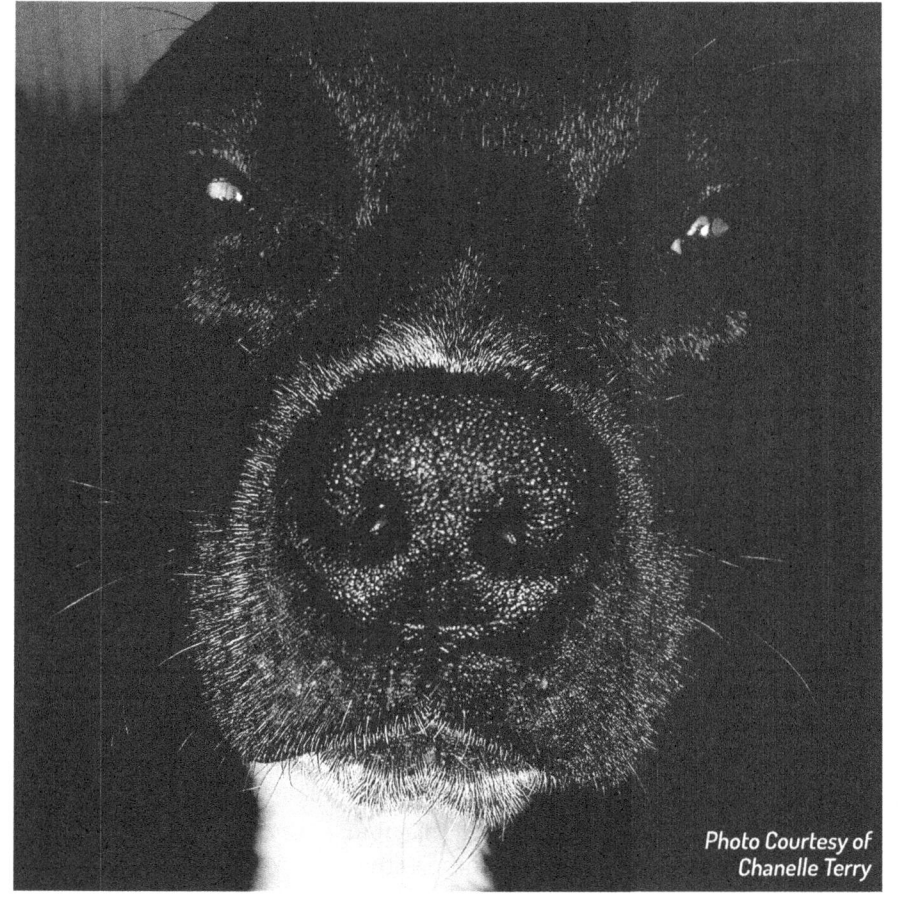

Photo Courtesy of Chanelle Terry

to develop cataracts. Carriers of the gene, which have one healthy gene and one cataract gene, will not go on to develop cataracts, but regardless they should not be bred from.

Cataracts are not painful, so many owners just choose to leave them and live with a blind dog. Many dogs do exceptionally well in life blind, as long as you don't move furniture around in the house and keep them on a lead for walks. Staffordshire Bull Terriers are also clever enough to learn difficult commands such as stop, turn back, slowly, and step. These will greatly aid them in staying out of trouble when they cannot see where they are going.

For owners who wish to treat their Staffie's cataracts, whole lens replacements are a surgical option. It is a complicated and fiddly surgery, and therefore it is only performed by veterinary ophthalmologists.

Skin Allergies

A common condition that Staffies suffer from is skin allergies. This is a frustrating, lifelong condition to treat, and there is no cure. But the good news is that once the allergy has been identified, it can be managed very well.

Allergies manifest in several different ways. The most common is itchy skin, usually in the belly, groin, armpit, and paw regions. The ear canals also can become inflamed and in more rare cases the bowel can become upset too, leading to diarrhea. There doesn't appear to be a pattern between the different allergens and different areas which become inflamed on the body, but rather it varies on each individual basis. Allergens can include food proteins (such as chicken, beef etc.), environmental allergens (such as grass, pollen etc.), and insect allergies (such as mites, fleas etc.). It is uncommon that a dog is just allergic to one thing, and usually several allergens are involved. Discovering which are the culprits is a process of elimination. There is the option for blood tests to be performed to investigate the reaction to different allergens, but these tests can be expensive as well as non-specific and inconclusive in their results. Nevertheless, in some cases, the results can be helpful for allergen avoidance or creation of a vaccination against the allergies.

Apart from development of allergen vaccines, there are several treatment options for managing allergies. The first is providing medications which bring down the inflammation in the skin through decreasing the immune response to the allergens. Most commonly steroid drugs are used, which can be administered in tablet, injection, spray, or cream forms. Steroids are extremely effective, but come with side effects, such as increased hunger, increased thirst, and a strain on the liver. Other forms of medica-tions which act in a similar manner include immune suppressants, such as cyclosporine, and antihistamines, such as chlorphenamine.

There are also ways of managing the skin so that the skin barrier is in better health and doesn't become as inflamed. The mainstay of this treat-ment is supplementing with omega oils. When omega-3 and omega-6 are in a perfect 1:3 ratio, they develop significant anti-inflammatory effects. This happens because a hormone-type substance called PGE2 is normal-ly formed in the inflammatory process, but omega oils cause PGE3 to be formed instead, which is significantly less inflammatory. In addition to this, shampoos containing tea tree or oatmeal help to keep the skin clean and free of bacteria, which can cause secondary infections when the skin barrier is weak.

In general, Staffordshire Bull Terriers have very few health problems compared to other pedigree breeds, and this is probably due to the fact that they are less inbred than other breeds, and so the gene pool is much larger. Nevertheless, it is always useful to be aware of the diseases and con-ditions which they might develop so that if your Staffie does develop any symptoms, they can be addressed and treated sooner rather than later.

CHAPTER 14
Living with a Senior Dog

Living with a senior Staffordshire Bull Terrier is quite different from living with a younger Staffie. While you will still find he is exuberant in many ways, he is now likely to take life at a bit of a slower pace. To look after a senior dog requires a slight management change from you, as the owner, as well. Things such as diet, exercise, and health care must all be taken into account. This is the time in your Staffie's life when pet insurance is likely to be needed, as most elderly dogs will end up with some sort of ailment which requires multiple vet visits or chronic care. If you didn't start up pet insurance from a young age, then it is not too late; however, the insurance company is likely to charge higher premiums and a higher excess for a senior dog.

Diet

Diet is linked so closely to the general health of your Staffie, and therefore a diet appropriate to his life stage is important. Senior diets are widely available from most commercial brands, so finding a senior diet in a pet store or supermarket should not be difficult.

Senior diets differ from normal adult diets in several different ways. Firstly, most senior diets have a slightly lower calorific content. This is because as dogs get older, they also generally become less mobile and do not need as many calories to maintain the same amount of weight. Keeping your senior dog slim will benefit his health greatly, as an increased weight can lead to liver failure, diabetes, heart failure, and strain on the joints. Senior foods will usually have a higher fiber content to increase satiety and keep your Staffie feeling fuller for longer, without the need for the extra calories.

Senior diets also usually contain additional ingredients to keep up good heart, brain, and joint health. This is usually through adding ingredients high in omega oils, such as fish or seed-based oils.

Some senior diets may have slightly different quantities of certain minerals compared to food for younger dogs. For example, potassium and sodium are linked closely to the function of the kidneys, and frequently the kidneys are compromised in older dogs. Sometimes pet foods take this into account and change the mineral balance of the food.

Finally, as dogs get older, they often struggle more with eating food. This might be because of poor dental health, arthritis in the jaw, or simply increased pickiness. As a result, most senior foods are easier and more enticing to eat. This can be through either increased palatability and improved taste, or the texture being softer and therefore easier to chew.

Senior Wellness Checks

As your Staffie ages, your visits to the vet should be more frequent. This is important even if your Staffie does not have any issues. That way, any conditions are picked up very early in the course of the disease. An early diagnosis can be the difference between life and death at this age, and prompt treatment will ensure that you can maintain the health and quality of life of your Staffie.

A senior wellness check should be carried out every six months, for any dog over the age of eight years old. This will include a physical examination, checking the teeth, eyesight, heart, lungs, abdomen, and temperature of your Staffie. Depending on how the physical exam is, your vet may wish to carry out a blood test and blood pressure test, to fully understand your Staffie's internal health. This is a good idea to carry out every year in very senior dogs, as organs, such as the liver or kidneys, can deteriorate very quickly.

HELPFUL TIP
Mobility Issues

Thanks to their size and shape, Staffordshire Bull Terriers are prone to both the large-dog problems of hip or elbow dysplasia and the small-dog problem of luxating patellas. Arthritis can result from any of these conditions or just old age. Have a plan to help care for your Staffy's aching joints as it gets older.

Many insurance companies will be happy to cover the cost of senior wellness checks for elderly patients, but you should always read the fine print of your policy, as no two policies are the same.

Photo Courtesy of Emma Ceely

Arthritis

Unfortunately, arthritis is extremely common in elderly dogs. One in five dogs over the age of eight years old who don't have any symptoms at all, will have undiagnosed arthritis. Arthritis develops from an ongoing abnormal pressure on the joint. This can either be because the joint is abnormal and receiving normal pressure, or because the joint is normal but receiving continuous abnormal pressure.

As discussed in Chapter 13, Staffordshire Bull Terriers are a breed which is prone to elbow and hip dysplasia. This means they can have abnormal joints with a normal pressure being exerted on them, and therefore as a breed, they are at a higher risk for developing arthritis.

Arthritis is a whole joint disease, meaning that it is not just one aspect of the joint which is affected. During the course of the disease, the joint cartilage degrades, the subchondral bone becomes damaged, and the joint fluid becomes thinner. As a result, the joint begins to grate when it moves and causes considerable pain.

Even though you cannot reverse arthritis, the good news is that there are plenty of management options to ensure your old Staffie is moving comfortably. The first line treatment is non-steroidal anti-inflammatory medications. These are daily medications which work similarly to most over-the-counter pain medications which you can get from your local pharmacy.

However, it is important to always give your Staffie canine medication and not human medication.

In addition to medication, you may also consider giving your Staffie joint supplements. These are usually in the form of powders or capsules, and contain glucosamine, chondroitin, MSM, and/or green-lipped mussel. These ingredients contain the precursors for making cartilage, and so they help to maintain the cartilage from degrading any further. The ingredients also help to improve the viscosity of the joint fluid, which improves the lubrication of the joint.

Physical rehabilitation is also an excellent way of building strength and providing pain relief without the need for more drugs. This is beneficial, as all medications must be filtered out from the body via the liver or kidneys, and as a result, these organs will have strain placed on them. Physical rehabilitation can take three different forms; physiotherapy, hydrotherapy, and acupuncture.

Physiotherapy is a therapy which helps improve the function of muscles and general mobility. It is often used for orthopedic and neurological cases; however, the application of it can be endless. For arthritic cases, the muscles will not be being used properly since the joints are sore, and physiotherapy will help to rebuild the strength in them. There are several types of exercises which are commonly carried out in physiotherapy sessions. The first type of exercise is general massage. This improves blood flow. The mainstay of physiotherapy sessions is exercises which encourage movement and functional use of limbs or balance. This can be done by using inflatable exercise balls to lean over, or inflatables to stand on, so that the body has to react and judge its position. This improves balance and tones postural muscles. Other common exercises include passive range of movement, which involves moving legs in a bicycle manner when they are lying on their side and not bearing weight, and exercises such as sit to stand, and weaving in and out of cones.

Another popular rehabilitation therapy for arthritis is hydrotherapy. This is more than just an expensive swimming session. Hydrotherapy is usually carried out by canine hydrotherapists, veterinary physiotherapists, or veterinary nurses, all of whom will have had extensive training. A hydrotherapy session will not be in a general swimming pool. Usually, there will be a purpose-built pool and underwater treadmill, specifically for canine hydrotherapy. Floats will often be used to aid dogs to stay in a good position in the water, and toys may also be brought out to encourage a positive experience. Hydrotherapy is most commonly used for dogs that need to build up muscle without putting stress on other anatomical parts of the body.

Finally, an excellent form of pain relief without medication is acupuncture. There are two types of acupuncture: Chinese and Western. Chinese is still widely practiced; however, the explanation of the therapy is now fairly outdated. There have been some major scientific advancements in the acupuncture world, which has given rise to Western acupuncture. It is now known that acupuncture works through stimulation of nerves, rather than by the flow of energy through meridians. There are many nerves in the body, some of which travel as bundles. These nerve bundles are thick, and can be targeted at certain points by acupuncture needles. If stimulated by a needle, the body will release a large amount of endorphin, which is like a natural morphine. This causes profound pain relief, as well as relaxation, minor sedation, improved blood flow, and a general happy feeling.

Not all vets will be able to offer acupuncture, hydrotherapy, or physiotherapy, but they are usually happy to refer patients to professionals who offer these services as complementary therapies to improve the quality of life of arthritic dogs.

Dementia

Until fairly recently, it was widely accepted that dogs lost some cognitive function as they aged; however, there is now a recognized condition called Canine Cognitive Dysfunction. This is very similar to dementia in humans. So, if you find your elderly Staffie is not the dog he used to be, there is a strong possibility that this is what he is suffering from.

The most common symptoms of CCD are dullness, lethargy, aimless wandering, urinating or defecating in abnormal areas when previously housebroken, and waking up at unusual times in the night.

Even though there is no cure to CCD, there is excellent medication available from your veterinarian. This medication improves the blood flow to the brain, which enables it to receive more oxygen and function better. You may find that this medication will give your old Staffie a whole new lease on life.

Organ Deterioration

With aging bodies come aging organs, and the four organs which take the most strain are the heart, lungs, liver, and kidneys.

The heart is a large muscle which pumps blood to the lungs and around the body. As the blood passes the lungs, it absorbs oxygen. This is then pumped to the rest of the body, and used by cells along with glucose, which is also carried by the blood. As a by-product, carbon dioxide is produced, which the blood then carries back to the lungs to be expelled from the body. Inside the heart are several valves to prevent backflow of blood. As dogs get older, these valves can become leaky and cause a turbulent flow of blood. This requires the heart to pump harder to move the same amount of blood around the body, and as a result the heart becomes enlarged. Catching heart disease early is important to stop further deterioration of the heart, and there are many medications available which improve the pumping function.

The liver is an organ linked closely to the digestive system. It has many uses including production of bile, which helps to digest fats, and filtration of toxins out of the body. Elderly animals with liver failure may have yellow gums and eyes, known as jaundice, as well as feel sick and have a poor appetite. There can be many reasons for liver disease, but in elderly dogs it is usually related to fibrosis, scarring, or cancer. While there are not very many medications available to treat liver disease, there are several supplements on the market which improve the function of the liver. In addition to this, a change in food to a food lower in protein will reduce the strain on the liver to process this.

The kidneys are a pair of organs linked to the bladder. Their main function is to filter waste and produce urine, but they also play many other roles. They are vitally important at regulating blood pressure and mineral balances, and they also play a role in the production of red blood cells. Needless to say, if they are not functioning well, then they can make your Staffie very sick. Deteriorating kidneys should be looked out for on senior wellness blood tests, as if you wait for clinical symptoms, the kidneys are already over 70% destroyed. There are many different medications which your veterinarian can prescribe to manage kidney disease; however, they are all targeting the symptoms and not the root cause. Once the kidneys are damaged, they are hard to restore.

Finally, there is a condition of the lungs called "old dog lungs." It is likely that if your Staffie is a senior dog, he may have some degree of this. It is completely normal, and even though it can cause the lungs to not function as well as they used to, they generally cause no harm. "Old dog lungs" occur when the lungs begin to fibrose and lose their elasticity. This makes them potentially more susceptible to inhaled allergens and bacteria. If listened to through a stethoscope, they will sound louder than usual. There is no need to treat elderly lungs, but it is important to be vigilant and seek medical attention quickly if you have an old dog with a lung infection, as your dog may be worse affected by it than if he was younger.

Loss of Senses

You are not alone if you have an old Staffie who is blind or deaf. These are two senses which are commonly lost later in life.

All eyes change with age, and it is usual to see a clouding over of the pupil. This can be due either due to cataracts or nuclear sclerosis. To the naked eye, both look very similar, and just because the pupil is becoming cloudy, it doesn't mean that the dog cannot see.

Nuclear sclerosis is simply a condensing of the components that make up the lens, and dogs can see through this. Cataracts, on the other hand, also affect the lens, but they are completely opaque and will lead to blindness of the dog. A veterinarian will be able to distinguish between the two by looking into the eye with an ophthalmoscope. As discussed in Chapter 13, cataracts are a common finding in Staffordshire Bull Terriers, and they don't always only happen in old age.

If a dog becomes blind, it is usually a slow process, which gives the owner time to start training useful commands, such as "wait," "slowly," and "step."

Many dogs will also lose their hearing, and because there are very few tests that can be done to assess hearing in pets, the extent to which an individual has lost its hearing is somewhat subjective. The owner might start to think the dog is becoming naughty and not responding to commands, but actually the dog just has not heard the command. When teaching commands as a puppy, it is a good idea to also teach a hand signal, so that they will also respond to this when they can no longer hear. For their safety, in open or public spaces, it is a good idea to keep the dog on a leash, as their recall will no longer be existent.

Bladder Control

Loss of bladder control may seem degrading to you; however, to your Staffie it is simply an inconvenience. Sadly, it does happen more frequently with older age, and determining the root cause is important to ensure appropriate treatment is provided.

As discussed in Chapter 12, spaying your Staffie prior to the first season can increase the risk of urinary incontinence, as the urinary sphincter which closes the bladder will not have a good tone to it. This is highly influenced by estrogen, so if your Staffie was spayed prior to her first season, there is a chance that the sphincter will become leaky later in life. Treatment for this is an effective daily tablet or syrup which replaces the hormone.

This can easily be confused with urinary incontinence for neurological reasons. The nerves that tell the sphincter to close originate at the level of the lower spine, and so arthritis of the spine, slipped discs, or other spinal issues can lead to urinary incontinence too. Treatment for this usually requires a veterinary neurologist to diagnose exactly what is wrong with the spine and treat the root cause.

Photo Courtesy of Rachel Marquis.

Saying Goodbye

For most owners, there will be a time when you have to consider whether your Staffie's quality of life has deteriorated so much that it would be a kinder option to put him to sleep. This is a difficult decision for any owner, and not one that should be taken without much careful thought. There are several aspects that will indicate that your Staffie's quality of life is deteriorating, and you can judge these aspects with several simple questions:

1. Is your Staffie's tail still regularly wagging?

2. Does your Staffie still want to interact with you?

3. Is your Staffie still eating well?

4. Can he still perform normal day-to-day activities?

If you come to the conclusion that it is the time to consider putting your Staffie to sleep, then your veterinarian can sensitively perform the procedure. The injection is simply an overdose of anesthetic, which will cause your Staffie to slip away into a deep sleep, before the heart stops. It is usually a peaceful procedure, and your Staffie will not feel any pain or worry about it.

The injection can be given at the vet clinic, at your house, or in your car at the vet practice. The important thing is that it is done where your dog is comfortable and peaceful, so that it will go as smoothly as possible. After it has been done, you will usually have the option of having your Staffie cremated or taking him home to bury.

It is always a difficult decision to make to put your Staffie to sleep; however, afterward you should try to focus on all the amazing times you had with your Staffie, his infectious smile, and how much joy he has brought to your life. This is a time to celebrate his life, instead of mourning his passing.

ACKNOWLEDGMENTS

I would like to dedicate this book to the first Staffie that I had a real connection with, Chunk. Many years ago, my mother used to volunteer to transport dogs. They were usually dogs who had been on their last days at rescue shelters, being transported to foster homes to give them a bit longer to find a permanent loving home. One day, she came home with this crazy dark brown Staffie, who was beyond exuberant. Unfortunately, he was partially sighted and so his exuberance was completely chaotic. As a result, he briefly adopted the name Clunky, rather than Chunk.

When it came to the night, his hyperactivity converted to nervous energy. I couldn't imagine what he must have been going through; a change in circumstance, people he didn't know, an unfamiliar face, and no way to see any of it. I slept on the floor with him that night, and gradually throughout the night, he crept closer and closer to me to finally cuddle up next to me. He eventually went on to be taken in by an understanding foster home, and received the veterinary treatment he needed for his eyes, and the good news is, his sight was restored.

Before meeting Chunk, I had a completely incorrect view of Staffordshire Bull Terriers. I have come to know and love them for being kind, caring, soft dogs, who are full of energy and joy.

Finally, as always, I would like to extend my thanks to my long-time editor, Clare Hardy, who does an exceptional job going through all my written work. Her input is invaluable. She has continuously provided me with incredible support, and I can't think of anyone else I would rather work with!

Made in the USA
Las Vegas, NV
03 October 2024